YOGA

and

LIVING SKILLS

Sophia Brandjes

Publisher
Gerald Brandjes
P.O. Box 89, Hornsby, N.S.W. 2077

Typesetting by:
Stewart Printing, 2 Ashley Lane, Hornsby, N.S.W. Australia.
Printed by:
MacArthur Press Pty. Ltd., Parramatta, N.S.W.

National Library of Australia Catalogue Card no. and
ISBN 0 7316 1675 8. First published 1987.

Caricature drawings
by Greg Richardson.

Cover design & figure drawings in
Part 3 by Ros Blackburn.

YOGA

and

LIVING SKILLS

I have often found acknowledgements in books rather amusing. You probably know the ones I am referring to: "My heartfelt thanks to my husband without whose help and support this book would never have been written." Now I find myself wanting to write the near identical thing! So here goes. . .

I am very fortunate to have such a talented and artistic mate. Gerald is responsible for the cover design and the captions which initiated the caricature drawings. Thank you Gerald for your love and confidence – thank you for being you.

Then I feel the need to mention my sister Cora who read the (very) rough manuscript, who gave me heaps of handy helpful hints and whose assistance and enthusiasm carried me through, as well as my dear friend Walter, who read the same manuscript and who suggested invaluable grammatical improvements. Thank you dear people!

Many thanks to my two favourite Yogis, Michael Volin and Howard Kent for their kind words and support.

A thank you to my daughters Cora, Alice and Jane and my grandchildren Anthony, Luke and Emily for their caring attitude and understanding while suffering my benign neglect during this past year.

My thanks to my friend Frances Plummer who managed to take such a lovely photograph of such an un-photogenic subject!

Finally, my gratitude to the many students who have come to me in trust and from whom I have learned so much.

Sophia Brandjes
Thornleigh – N.S.W. 1987

Every new day should be a celebration – a real "Birthday".

PREFACE

In the past twenty years more and more people have become aware that we are standing at the "turning point" of our history. The whole process could be described as an "inner" revolution, from a re-evaluation of old values, the dissatisfaction with many social issues and economical structures, to a growing awareness of the importance of ecological balance, conservation, open mindedness towards metaphysics and a willingness to have a "second look" at the native approach to health and healing. The "witch doctor revisited" trend is not only the reserve of mystically orientated people but has become a part of scientific research.

Perhaps the most profound aspect of our changing times is the ever-growing interest in Alternative Medicine and the Holistic Health Movement, leading to the emergence of "new truths" substituting orthodox beliefs and ideas. This book is a valuable contribution to this end. It is a well-written and easy to understand work presenting the healing aspects of Yoga.

The author, a Yoga practitioner herself, stresses the point that Yoga is not only a form of oriental gymnastics with the aim of achieving extreme suppleness and the ability to "tie oneself in knots", but rather a system to UNTIE the knots, on physical, mental and spiritual levels, through the practice of relaxation, breathing exercises and meditation.

The main theme of this book is how to help Nature restore the balance we call health. Commonsense and constructive thinking play an important part in this process. People suffering from debilitating ailments such as Parkinson's Disease and Multiple Sclerosis could be greatly benefitted by studying and following the techniques outlined in this book.

Michael Volin
Adelaide 1987.

FOREWORD

One of the biggest drawbacks to the effective development of yoga, is the number of teachers who really have a half-hearted attitude towards it. They have kept their gaze on the ground, rather than 'lifting their eyes unto the hills'. Their yoga is 'practical' in the sense that it is hum-drum.

The truth is that yoga is nothing if it is not inspirational. The glory comes from looking and stretching upwards. Of course, we'll topple over. When we do we must pick ourselves up, dust ourselves down – and start all over again. Anyone who is looking for an easy passage of life, should not start practising yoga. It is a self-discipline, it is difficult and from time to time we will come near to despair. Yet if we persevere we will find we have moved forward. Can any other approach to life offer us as much?

Some followers of various religions will say that basic faith is all we need. Yet, understood in the right way, there is a depth of truth in the saying, "God helps those who help themselves." The sages of yoga were men of great faith, yet they saw the need to couple their faith with practice.

There is, of course, immense value in studying the lives and following great men. In India sages of yoga grow in abundance – the good, the bad and the indifferent. All too often they are called gurus and are regarded virtually as manifestations of God. Their lives appear to be very different from those of people in the West.

India, therefore, offers us the yoga of the illuminated man. The West offers the yoga of experience – experience hammered out in the rush and stress of our pressurised society.

Sophia Brandjes is an excellent example of the latter type of yoga. Her life has been by no means free of problems and she makes no secret of the difficulties she has faced. So her yoga is not the yoga of pious words and high-flown experiences, it is the yoga which she finds works for us, even when we are beset by problems which are always puzzling and which often appear to be insoluable.

This is why her book is so valuable. It is deliberately unpretentious, but that is a matter for praise, not criticism. Nevertheless, at no time does she bowdlerise yoga, simplify it to inanity. She offers the whole subject, shorn of pompousness. For this she deserves our heartfelt thanks.

In the course of the book, Sophia emphasises the value of a good teacher. No book can replace the importance of personal contact. Yet many people may not find a teacher who really appeals to them: even if they must then perforce work alone, the straightforward approach of this work will be of immense value to them. If they do find a teacher who is **sympatico**, then this book will be a valuable bonus.

HOWARD KENT
Yoga for Health Foundation
Ickwell Bury – Northill
Biggleswade – Bedfordshire · England 1987

INTRODUCTION

Why write this book? There are already so many books about Yoga, the power of the mind, positive thinking, healthy living, dietary advice and other such subjects, generally regarded as "non-popular" reading material. This mainly, because the information offered may call for a change of life style, which is usually not appreciated by people, free-wheeling happily downhill to become statistical evidence of increases in heart disease, cancer, nervous disorders, respiratory ailments and other unpleasant encounters of the same kind.

Yet, I feel, that amongst all this information there is, perhaps, a place for a book such as mine – a book mainly relating to personal experiences, pointing out how simple it is to enter and follow the Yoga path and to acquire the living skills some of us may have lost, or perhaps never possessed.

There is another reason for this book. This is, the need I feel to tell as many people as possible of the health and happiness which Yoga has given me.

This book therefore, is no in-depth study of Yoga and Yoga philosophy and is for the un-initiated as well as (I hope!) for those, who are quite familiar with the subject. For those, who are looking for a better life style and for those, who have the distinct feeling, that there must be more to life than what they have experienced so far – that there must be "something better than this".

Many books on Yoga give so much detailed information and depict Yogis in such extra-ordinary postures, that they scare people off rather than attract them. Their first reaction to that kind of book usually is: "This is not for me." "I could never do that anyway".

And yet Yoga is so much more than tying yourself into a physical knot or standing on your head. If anything, Yoga will "untie" all the physical and mental knots you may have! Yoga is a life style which can easily and without trauma, be integrated into your daily routine, without interfering with what might loosely be called "normal living". In fact, to be effective, Yoga must be **relevant** to your life.

Some might consider parts of this book light-hearted but I believe, that Yoga is often treated too solemnly. Yoga is about health, happiness, joy and laughter, about feeling good about yourself and others, about being able to cope, about balance in everything.

This I understand to be the essence of Yoga as it is the essence of balanced living.

I warned you not to take Yoga lessons by correspondence!

CHAPTER 1

HOW I BECAME INVOLVED

What are you doing Oma? My then two-year old grandson was bending over, craning his neck, trying to bring his little face close to mine.

Was it the first time he saw me in the head stand? Most probably not, but it must have been the first time it registered, that there was something unusual about a grandmother in upside-down position at 5.30 in the morning.

To react to his question by saying, that I was practising Yoga, would not have been the whole answer as involvement in Yoga and adopting a Yogic life style does not require standing on one's head. It requires living in an "upside-down" world while staying "level-headed".

I was a none too healthy, highly-strung, young mother of two daughters (4 and 1), when my husband Gerald suggested that I should take up Yoga. This is twenty seven years ago now, while we were living in New Zealand. I had never heard of Yoga before and would not have gone to find out what it was, if Gerald had not insisted, that I try it. Looking back, it was one of the best things I ever did! (I feel I did three "best things" in my life: getting marrried, having my three daughters and becoming involved in Yoga).

My first Yoga class was a very memorable one. Sir Paul Dukes was on a tour of New Zealand and conducted the session. Of course I had no idea in what august Yoga company I was that night. However, I did perceive that he was a very special person and felt enormously motivated through meeting him. So much so, that it is true to say, that from that night onwards I practised some Yoga every day of my life.

At first I did very little – only the postures and movements I could remember from the classes. But soon my repertoire increased, I began to feel better in myself and became more supple.

I was born and grew up in Holland, the eldest child in a family of six girls and one boy. Our childhood was a busy one, at least this seems so in retrospect. We had all the usual childhood diseases, probably because there were so many of us. What the one did not catch an other would bring home, after which we would all have the illness in turn! I also had the more unusual ones such as diptheria (twice), malaria and pneumonia – the diptheria and pneumonia landed me in hospital, as this happened at a time when anti-biotics had not been discovered.

I married at twenty-two and was often sick during the first ten years of my marriage. One cross I seemed to have to bear was cystitis and another a recurring back problem. Add to this, that my equilibrium was very easily shaken and you have a fair idea of my physical and mental state. In fact, most years when filling out our tax forms and adding up our medical expenses, I topped the doctor's bills out of all five of us!.

I am telling you this for a reason. (There must be a good one, because there is little more boring than reading about someone else's illnesses). Truth is, that since I started practising Yoga, my health has improved out of sight, so that now I see a doctor once a year for a Pap smear and a check-up.

When I look back on the first years of my Yoga practice, I can't help smiling. Some Yogis may even throw up their hands in horror. Of course, it was not really Yoga the way I understand it today, Although I did the postures, it was more like physical exercises. However, it was the beginning of a discipline: every morning practice – once a week to class.

The family got used to stepping over me as I lay on the lounge floor early every morning and many a time Gerald got on to his knees to kiss me good-bye before going to work.

When the girls became older, they did their piano practice before leaving for school and I would supervise their study, giving them directions from the floor!

Even the grand children are used to waiting for their breakfast till Oma (Dutch for grandmother) has finished her Yoga practice.

In fact, they think, that all grandparents do this every morning. Grandparents, yes, because Gerald, after being seriously ill with pneumonia a few years ago, finally adopted the life style too and practises most mornings.

As far as our daughters are concerned, Alice, our second daughter, had no choice. She had asthma as a young girl and I made her practise every morning as soon as she woke up. She has not had an attack since she was sixteen and she is twenty seven now. Our youngest daughter, Jane, came to meditation when she was very sick last year. I will touch upon this later in the book. Our eldest daughter, Cora, although very interested in Yoga, has not made it part of her life.

Yoga does not have to mean sudden and drastic changes to one's life. We travelled a lot and lived in different countries.

There were many social obligations and I have had to cope under difficult circumstances. I am convinced, that Yoga gave me the energy and stamina to handle most situations.

It took a long time before it dawned on me that there was more to Yoga than physical movement and I became interested in the mental and spiritual side of it. I began to ask questions, read books on the subject, went to seminars, finally enrolled in a Yoga teachers training course and began to teach.

The changes which took place came slowly and gradually and I feel that this is good. If you try to change overnight, you are bound to encounter stress in yourself and opposition from those around you. By a gradual process, you can adopt changes and make them part of you without any trauma.

One change which comes with Yoga, is discipline. Find the self-discipline to practise every morning and you will find, that this discipline permeates your daily life.

Another change is diet. It becomes much easier to refuse that cream cake at morning tea time. I would feel a fool eating one after practising in the morning! I became more food conscious and slowly changed the fare at mealtimes. I feel this benefitted the whole family.

I became a vegetarian sixteen years ago and I have felt great benefit from this. As with the practice of Yoga, I left the girls free to decide for themselves. They have drifted in and out of vegetarianism but on the whole they eat little or no meat, neither does Gerald.

It was very interesting to observe the consequence of having no longer meat in my diet. About three months after I had ceased eating meat, I noticed that I was suddenly more supple – all the joints seemed to move much more freely.

Although I had practised daily for eleven years, the change was dramatic. So much so, that not only I noticed it, but also those around me. The saying "One is what one eats", was certainly true for me.!

Most importantly, I feel, that Yoga has assisted me in finding peace within myself. It has helped me to "centre" and to remain calm in difficult situations. It has taught me to accept myself with all my short-comings and limitations and at the same time given me direction to make the most of my given talents and opportunities.

CHAPTER 2

YOGA AS A LIFE STYLE

Yoga is a philosophy, a life style – it is not a religion and as such does not interfere with the religion of one's choice. In fact, it has been found to deepen one's personal religious experience. Yoga is a system, which is centuries old and is a way of breathing, thinking and working, which is most suitable for the twentieth century with its problems of increasing pollution and stress.

Yoga aims at a healthy mind in a healthy body or as it is put in Latin: "Mens sana in corpore sano", a sound mind in a sound body. In order to achieve this, Yoga works on the body first. We all know from personal experience, that if anything physical is bothering us; a headache – a pain in the back, all we seem to be able to think about is that particular part of the body and of how miserable we feel.

Peace of mind is very hard to attain under such circumstances. One has to be a Saint to be cheerful when the body lets us down and who wants to be a Saint nowadays? However, when the body is at its highest peak of physical health, we can forget about it and concentrate on and concern ourselves with the important things in life.

We are living inside our physical bodies, which can either hamper us or allow our spirits to be set free.

On a different plane the Yogis say, that the body is the temple of the soul and give this as the motivation for taking care of the body. If you cannot accept the concept of "soul" use your own substitution "I", "true self", "essential me".

Look at it this way: the body is a very intricate system with most parts depending on each other. Many people would not treat their sewing machine or circular saw the way they treat their bodies. And yet the sewing machine and the saw are replaceable, whereas we are issued only one body during our life time.

Although the medical profession seems to be going into the spare parts business, these surgical procedures are not always successful. Spare parts are at best **second best!**

Some people act as unintentional suicides through unhealthy diets, smoking cigarettes, use of alcohol or taking of drugs. Their bodies are already breaking down before they reach maturity. They then begin to feel that life is a drag, that they are physically and mentally not up to it, that they can't cope and they lose the purpose in and zest for life.

Of course Yoga is no miracle cure. It takes time and effort: you get out of it what you put into it. As they say: "There are no free lunches"! But do try it – you too will find, that life can be beautiful.

Yoga teaches detachment. When I was first introduced to this concept, I thought: "No way!" I felt, that life was about being AT-tached not DE-tached – identifying attachment with caring and loving. Of course I did not comprehend what was meant by detachment. Indeed we must love and care and through Yoga we have more energy and time to care for those around us, because we learn to find our equilibrium and hence can devote our energy to the welfare of others.

As I understand it, detachment means that our happiness does not depend on people or material possessions. In other words, while we possess certain things we enjoy them but if for some reason they were no longer there, this would not affect our happiness. Likewise with people. We love our family, both immediate and extended – we love our friends. We know however, that they will not always be with us – some will die before we do and others will leave us to pursue their own interests and to fulfil their ambitions. We learn to understand and accept this through detachment, we will cultivate an attitude of "it was good while it lasted". This way our greatest source of grief is taken away from us.

There will be no real sadness at farewells. We will understand, that we are saying "good-bye" because there was a "hello" – the meeting is in fact the beginning of the farewell. We should be grateful for the privilege of having been able to spend time together and not spoil it by sadness at parting. I feel that we never quite part at all.

Those who are leaving us for good have in some way become part of us through our having known them. Those who are just moving away can always be contacted by letter, phone or through visits. As for our children, although we know intellectually, that we only bring them up to make them independent, parting from them is the greatest wrench of all. Kahlil Gibran, a Lebanese philosopher and painter, who lived nearly all his life in the United States, where he died in 1931 at the age of forty eight, writes in his book *"The Prophet"* when asked to speak about children, and I quote in part:

Your children are not your children.
They are the sons and daughters of Life's longing for itself.
They come through you but not from you,
And though they are with you yet they belong not to you.

You may give them your love but not your thoughts,
For they have their own thoughts.
You may house their bodies but not their souls,
For their souls dwell in the house of tomorrow,
which you cannot visit, not even in your dreams.
You may strive to be like them, but seek not to make them like you.
For life goes not backward nor tarries with yesterday.
You are the bows from which your children as living arrows are sent forth.

Detachment teaches true love. When we love truly, we can let go. Holding on is selfishness – letting go is love, is detachment.

Detachment also teaches, that we are alone, but not lonely – that we are part of all there is. Again, then we can let go – we wont have the need to hold on.

Ideally and to have maximum effect, we should practise Yoga daily. Students sometimes tell me, that they would like to do this, but that they have no time for it, So much time is wasted through being disorganised, through lack of discipline. Make every minute work for you – it does not return! It is not selfish to spend some time each day on yourself. On the contrary, you owe it to yourself – you will feel better for it and become a more pleasant person to have around.

Your daily practice does not have to take much time. Try to get up ten minutes earlier than you normally would. If you are living with others, try to be up before the rest of the group.

Taste the stillness – experience the newness of the day – see the sun rise. There is magic in this change from dark to light.

Early rising may be difficult at first. The secret is not to procrastinate when you hear the alarm go off. It is the first foot out of bed which is the most difficult – after that it is a breeze! If you really want to do something, make up your mind and do it! Don't become a "but-person". "I would like to do this, but...", "I would like to be slim, but...". "But-people" seldom do or achieve anything , they only wish they could.

Yoga is a way of overcoming suffering. It is directed to body and soul. The Yoga philosophy shows, that we are responsible for ourselves – it teaches us self-regulation and self-determination. Above all, it gives us courage.

Yoga brings us in balance with our environment. When we are not in balance, we create tension. There has to be harmony in all we undertake. Yoga is mind-directed – it balances the mind.

The mind motivates us. If we are not motivated, we will not do anything unless we are forced to. This is not a very mature state of affairs. It is the mind which directs us to study, exercise, walk, talk, not to smoke, not to drink alcoholic beverages, not to over-eat.

All and everything exists in the mind – both good and bad, positive and negative, joy and sadness, courage and fear, peace and turbulence, serenity and anxiety. **You** can choose which one it is going to be!

Begin by exercising the body slowly and gently, progressing at your own pace – your own tempo. Gradually your body demands will change, so that it will be no hardship for you to persevere with a certain diet, to catch up on your correspondence, to give up smoking, to be more patient, or whatever it is you would like to do or be. Adopt a Yoga practice which is **relevant to your life.**

Your daily practice will be like a celebration: Your body functioning as it should – a clean slate – fresh opportunities – a new day.

If beauty is in the eye of the beholder, why is there often so little beauty in the "I" of the beholder?

CHAPTER 3

I COULD NEVER DO THAT!

Let us face it – there are not too many people, who are perfectly healthy – who don't have a problem somewhere. In fact, there are no perfect people, we all have problems, we are all disabled to a degree, some more obviously than others. Some hide this better than others!

When discussing a positive approach to relieve or alleviate body and mind discomforts by applying a better health regimen, I invariably arrive at exercise and diet. And it is then that I often hear the remark: "I could never do that!".

It is truly amazing how many discomforts people are willing to suffer so long as they don't have to make changes to their lives, to their habits.

Especially, if one introduces Yoga as a means of improving the quality of life, the "I-could-never-do-that" reaction becomes a common catchcry.

It is often not understood, that even if you never master all asanas (postures), it does not matter at all. It is important that you try, that you make a start. The benefit is not in how far you go or how perfect the posture is; the benefit is in the trying and in the attention given to the trying.

Attentiveness is the heart of Yoga. Lack of attentiveness makes the asana collapse. Attentiveness is the therapy. YOGA IS THERAPEUTIC.

Look at it this way: if you are having problems today doing the most natural things like bending forward, walking properly, sitting with your back straight, imagine what you will be like in ten years time! Twenty years from now you may hardly be able to move – arthritis and stiffness of the joints and muscles may have well and truly set in.

Look around you. Many middle-aged people begin to find it increasingly difficult to do up their shoelaces or to pick up things from the floor. Their backs ache, they can no longer run, their stomach muscles are slack, resulting in pot bellies, their hip joints are so stiff, that when they walk, it looks as if they are pushing a wheelbarrow, their shoulders hunched, their heads are protruding from their necks. Not a pretty sight – not a pleasant condition to be in!

If this picture fits you to any degree at all, **don't despair!** Keep moving! Begin by doing some simple exercises at first. Especially the "Exercises to be done while lying in bed", which you can find in part 3 of the book, are extremely beneficial, particularly if done while lying on the floor. (A firm surface is very important).

Teaching Yoga to High School students made me aware of the fact that young people are often very stiff too – even those who are active in sports. One can't use the body the way it was designed to be used when the muscles attached to the skeleton no longer stretch. Observe a lion or a tiger in the Zoo, or even your own pet for that matter, before it becomes so domesticated that it too becomes arthritic. See the rippling of the muscles beneath the skin as the animal stretches and walks. See the movements in the shoulder and hip joint.

A body which moves well is a pleasure to behold – it is a pleasure to live inside a body which moves well!

Try exercising daily and if possible at the same time and place every day. Routine is important – the session becomes an essential part of your daily life. Your body begins to expect it, like having its face washed, its teeth brushed, its hair combed.

Determine what time of the day is most suitable for you: early in the morning before you start your day (ideal!), or when the little ones are having their nap, or before dinner after you return from work. Every day: same time, same place.

Find your weak spots and devote some time to them each day: weak spine, soft stomach muscles, incorrect posture. We are a world full of uncomfortable people through bad posture.

We should aim at flexibility of body and mind, avoiding stiffness of body and a "set" mind.

Remember, that each of us "became", when two cells combined. It was then, that our bodies began to evolve. Look at a healthy baby's body – it is beautiful and perfect. Nobody pities the baby; on the contrary, we exclaim about the shape of the fingers, the nose, the colour of the eyes – we can't look enough at this new little person. Why then should the adult body become something of an embarrassment, something to be hidden, something to be covered up?

Become aware of the beauty of the body – become aware of how it functions. It is a miracle and a mystery – it is a tool for learning.

During our Yoga practice we aim to use only the muscles needed to perform a certain movement or asana – the non-involved muscles remain relaxed. When the action is completed, the muscles involved should return to the relaxed state. Yoga works with the relaxed muscle. A relaxed muscle can stretch without risk of damage, a tense, taut muscle can very easily be injured.

There is no age limit. There is a Yoga practice for everyone, for every age and for every physical condition. You can always adapt.

Those who are on weight-reducing diets should certainly exercise. The gentle movements of Yoga will help break up fat deposits, revitalise the metabolism and tone the muscles. Unlike sports Yoga does not build muscles, it tones them. One can actually lose dimensions without losing weight.

Don't be too hard on yourself. Do your best – best is the best there is. There is no bester or bestest! Nothing more to do than your BEST.

Yoga is not something we do once a week – that is a start. Our Yoga practice should be relevant to our life. Yoga should be an integral part of it. We should "breathe" Yoga, "eat" Yoga, "feel" Yoga, "think" Yoga – BECOME IT, BE IT.

By considering the pleasures of the "healthy body", the improved lifestyle and caring, the coping mental condition, which flow from that, the self-created obstacle of "I-could-never-do-that", should be cleared out of the way.

Believe in yourself – be positive – of course "You CAN do that!".

CHAPTER 4

BREATH..... THE SOURCE OF LIFE

Breathing is the most natural function of the body. It is the first thing we do on entering this world and the last thing we do before leaving it.

It is the most important function of the body. We could live without food for a while – we could survive without water for less time than without food, but without the breath there would be no life. Breathing supplies the body with oxygen and rids it of carbon dioxide. However, there must be balance in our intake of oxygen and our output of carbon dioxide.

There are people who habitually hyperventilate (over breathe). They have a much greater input of oxygen and their level of carbon dioxide becomes too low. While we need oxygen in order to function properly, too much is detrimental to the body, as oxygen itself is a toxic substance. The same applies to carbon dioxide – this too is toxic, but essential for the body's proper functioning. We are a very finely balanced mechanism with the emphasis on "balanced". Without this balance we get into trouble.

Under breathing (hypoventilating) is equally detrimental to the body's state of health, as here again the balance between carbon dioxide and oxygen is affected. Hyperventilation is most commonly found in people, who are under constant stress, real or imagined, while hypoventilation is usually perceived in people who are already ill and are feeling hopeless and out of control.

That hyperventilation finally produces illness, is now more and more accepted. Symptoms such as chest pains, dizziness, palpitations, migraine, asthma, mental disorientation, memory lapses, numbness, sweating, visual disturbances as well as anxiety and panic states, phobias and symptoms which resemble stroke, heart attack and abdominal disorders, are now often accepted to be triggered off by faulty breathing.

The body is a system of combustion and of electricity. To combust the food we ingest, we need oxygen – to generate electricity, we need natural respiration.

We are an energy field and as such need constant replenishing as we use up our energy. We need to link into the universal energy system. Breathing links us into the cosmic energy field.

The problem is that most people would not know whether their breathing is impaired and even if they did, they would not know how to set about the restoration of the natural breath.

We all knew initially how to breathe correctly, unless we were born with particular respiratory problems. However, somewhere along the road of life we were dealt a blow, which we found hard to cope with. This upset our breathing pattern. If this is temporary only, there is little harm done. In fact we all hyperventilate at times. It is the body's natural response to stress or fright. It is when hyperventilating becomes habitual, that the damage of the body's functioning occurs.

What happens during natural breathing? The lungs are the organs which are used during respiration – they inflate during inhalation and deflate during exhalation. The lungs are situated in the chest, surrounded by the ribcage, while the diaphragm lies below the lungs, dividing the thoracic and abdominal cavities and is attached to the lower ribs at each side and to the breast bone and spine at the front and back.

For the lungs to function properly, the floating ribs have to be able to move freely outwards as they were designed to do, thereby assisting to stretch and flatten the diaphragm. When the ribs move inward again, the diaphragm returns to its original dome-like shape.

It seems a very natural and at the same time simple operation: Inhaling – the ribcage expands, thereby stretching the diaphragm and allowing the lungs to fill with air as they inflate; Exhaling – the ribcage contracts, the diaphragm returns to its original position, thereby squeezing the lungs clear of all air. What could be more simple?

And yet, observing what is being practised in the area of respiration, it appears that the variety of breathing patterns is endless, although they can all be placed either in the category of hyper- or hypoventilation.

From recent research it would seem that our breath is the mirror of our mental state. It reflects the way we think and feel and is especially influenced by our emotional state. Why is it, that specifically our breathing seems to be affected by our life experiences?

Deep breathing becomes automatic when in stress...

Our emotional state has immediate physical consequences. We have all experienced this: a fright makes us hold our breath or take a sudden large gulp of air. It makes our heart race and all our muscles contract. On the other hand, a feeling of hopelessness and of being out of control, influences our posture – the shoulders hunch up, the chest caves in, we slouch and thereby physiologically impair our breathing capacity. Furthermore, feeling like that, we don't really want to take deep breaths anyway, as every effort seems too much. Then observe what the result is of a feeling of defiance. This makes us push out our chest, "rigidifying" our ribcage, which then loses the capacity to expand and contract freely.

There are two kinds of natural breathing: the energising breath, employed while working and playing and the relaxed breath, which is used when the body and mind are at rest.

When we practise the **relaxed breath,** the posture should be comfortable, the spine straight, the chest open as a slouching posture hampers any correct breathing. The shoulders, arms and hands should be relaxed, the latter lying comfortably in the lap – one hand resting in the other, palms up. Sometimes resting the hands on a cushion placed in the lap, or supporting the lumbar area by a small cushion, adds to the body comfort of the person.

Lying down on the floor is ideal as the body is supported. Place the body in a straight line, head in line with the spine, chin toward the chest, arms away from the body with the palms of the hands turned upwards, feet twelve to eighteen inches apart with the ankles soft and the feet falling outward.

If you are uncomfortable lying like this through spinal problems, place one or two pillows under the bent knees, resting the legs. If the head tends to fall back, arching the back of the neck and making the chin jut upward, you can place a small cushion under the head. (see part 3)

During relaxed breathing we "do" as little as possible. We let the breath "happen". Rather than being involved in the physical process of breathing, we now only observe this process. The chest is quite still as the abdomen will gently rise and fall.

Rise on the inhalation – fall on the exhalation. Not by means of any action on our part, but by means of the phrenic nerves, which govern the diaphragm. This process will slow the rate of breathing down from the usual fourteen to sixteen breaths per minute to four to six per minute.

It is essential that the body is relaxed during this breathing process and not involve itself with the mechanics of it. This in turn would lead to tension, which would defeat the whole purpose of the relaxed breath being the restoration of the natural breathing process.

During the practice of the **energising breath**, there is both physical and mental involvement. It takes thought and effort to expand and contract the ribcage, while holding the abdomen still. Of course with practice, this will become quite natural and effortless.

While during the relaxed breath the abdomen moves up and down, during the process of energising breathing, the abdomen is still and controlled as is the top part of the chest. Only the area of the floating ribs moves outward on the inhalation and inward on the exhalation.

Holding the abdominal wall still and controlled has quite a few physiological consequences. When the diaphragm flattens on the inhalation, while the abdominal wall remains controlled, the volume of the abdominal cavity is decreased and pressure is put on the abdominal organs, squeezing and massaging them. On the exhalation the reverse happens; the diaphragm returns to its original dome-like shape and the pressure in the abdomen is released, allowing fresh blood to flush the abdominal organs.

In the area of the chest a similar situation arises only in reverse. On inhaling, the chest expands and the diaphragm flattens out toward the abdomen, releasing the pressure in the chest thereby allowing the air to flow into the lungs. While exhaling the diaphragm returns upward and the thoracic cavity returns to its original volume, when the floating ribs move inward again, thereby squeezing the lungs clear of all air as well as massaging the heart. So we squeeze and release..., squeeze and release alternatively in the thoracic and abdominal cavity.

"What about the full Yoga breath", I hear you ask. "What is wrong with extending and contracting the abdominal wall when breathing in and out?" When we use this technique (and it is a technique – it is not the natural way of breathing), the volume of the abdomen remains the same whether breathing in or out, because although the diaphragm descends, causing the volume of the abdomen to decrease, this is offset by the extension of the abdominal wall. Hence inside the abdomen there is NO change. As a consequence a large quantity of stagnant blood wil gorge and congest the abdominal organs.

To sum up:

1.– There is constant pressure difference in the thoracic and abdominal area (as well as between the two), during diaphragmatic breathing. This aids the blood circulation from the abdominal area to the heart and lungs and consequently the total blood circulation as there is no stagnation anywhere. That this lightens the task of the heart considerably is obvious.

This is what we are trying to achieve: a slow, strong heartbeat and a deep, slow breath. The one does not exist without the other.

2.– We are no longer speaking of "full Yoga breath" or abdominal breathing, but of diaphragmatic breathing with abdominal control. This does not imply a tightness, a contraction of the abdomen. This would impede diaphragmatic breathing and we would be in the same position as the tense person, who only breathes high in the chest.

3.– A healthy body depends on an adequate and balanced supply of oxygen and nutrients being carried to all body cells by the blood stream while at the same time waste matter is being removed from the cells. Passing through the lungs, the blood should be ingested with a fresh supply of oxygen while disposing of carbon dioxide. However, when breathing is impaired or shallow (through smoking, lack of exercise, incorrect posture, etc.) the lungs no longer function properly. As a result the cells become starved of oxygen and nutrients while becoming clogged with waste matter. We will begin to feel uneasy – we will experience a feeling of dis-ease and become diseased.

One more detail of interest, which perhaps may be mentioned before I leave the physiological benefits of the natural way of breathing is the following: Natural breathing increases and decreases the brain volume, thereby massaging the brain mass. Also when we are breathing slowly and deeply, slowing the respiration down to six or less breaths per minute, our endocrinal glandular system works at its fullest capacity, thereby balancing the hormonal flow in the body. When the hormonal secretion is balanced, our sense of well-being is enhanced.

All this just because we have learned to breathe the natural way! We must not forget, that although breathing is totally automatic and autonomic – we do not have to think about it it continues anyway – it is also the only body process, which can be manipulated and brought under complete control of the mind. Consider it: we can breathe slowly or quickly, we can breathe deeply or shallowly, we can hold the breath in or out. **It is obvious, that we are meant to use this facility as a tool to maintain a physical and mental state of well-being.**

During sports or exertion the breathing is often not rhythmical, but hurried and jerky. The amount of oxygen inhaled, is immediately consumed and dissipated. Hence after an hour's tennis or running, we often feel tired. On the other hand an hour's Yoga practice renews and regenerates because of the restoring influence of rhythmical deep breathing and the gentle exercises for body and mind.

There is a direct relationship between the amount of environmental, physical and emotional/mental stress we suffer and the way in which we breathe. When I say "suffer", I mean to indicate that something which presents itself as stress to me, is not necessarily experienced as stress by others and vice versa. It is our REACTION to a situation, which creates the stress and not the ACTUAL TRIGGER.

Breathing is the balance sheet of our body's activities.
Breathing is the balance sheet of our emotions.
Breathing is the balance sheet of our mental state.

Energy is central to living. We are part of the universe – therefore we are part of the universal energy. This energy does not increase or diminish – it is constant. The universal energy should flow unimpeded through us – it is ours by right! When through stress we become tense, our breathing is affected and we begin to feel uneasy, we experience a sensation of dis-ease and become diseased. Absolutely everything is based on the free flow of energy. OUR LIFE DEPENDS ON IT!

Yoga teaches that respiration is more than an intake of oxygen and an expulsion of carbon dioxide. Through respiration we are in communion with the Life Force, the Essence of Life. Therefore, little breath – little life; insufficient breath – insufficient life; full breath – full life.

Don't re-enforce stress by rehashing it: "I was so mad!" "I was so upset!" If you need to talk about it, do it once, perhaps twice but if you find yourself doing it a third time, stop and consider what you are doing. You will realise that you are experiencing the same tension and distress as you did when you were in the original situation thereby enforcing the stress experience. **Learn** from an experience and then **move on.** Stress affects the immune system, causing imbalance in our hormone levels.

Respiration puts us in charge, the feeling of helplessness disappears. We need not go outside ourselves for help and assistance. (We may have to occasionally, but not on a regular basis.) Please try it – it is so simple. You have nothing to lose and everything to gain.

When we breathe rhythmically, we become attuned to the rhythm of the universe. We establish a sense of one-ness with it. The feeling of separate-ness disappears and with it fear, loneliness, doubt and despair. Feeling at one with the universe, we begin to understand how we are part of all there is, how we are truly part of creation. We begin to comprehend fully, that we are not an island but that all we do, or omit to do, will have a bearing on everyone and everything. With the sense of "being part of all there is" with the disappearance of loneliness, will come a sense of responsibility and belonging. This will result in the disappearance of the feeling of futility and uselessness and we'll become more directed as we begin to grasp the Grand Design.

We will learn to be patient with others but more importantly with ourselves as we begin to see the insignificance of most of our worries and fears.

We begin to understand that we waste an enormous amount of energy on needless worrying, energy much better employed elsewhere. As we begin to feel better physically through improved breathing, we will also become more robust mentally. We will acquire a zest for life, rather than dreading each new day.

Of course all these things take time. As it is with the breath so it is with the postures and movements: Make a beginning – a commitment. One day at a time – forward looking, trusting that you can and will improve. Meanwhile, you will be experiencing the joy of improved health and an increased sense of well-being.

If we want to achieve something, we have to work constantly and consistently, keeping our goal and purpose before our mind's eye. All we need to reach that goal is patience, perseverence, a positive attitude and correct breathing.

CHAPTER 5

NOT TOO MUCH DISTRESS ABOUT STRESS

To wish not to experience stress is literally to wish to be dead.

All movement requires tension which means stress of some muscle and/or organ. Tension is a totally natural phenomenon and as such does no harm to the body. In fact, if we became totally immobile, we would do real harm to ourselves as muscles and bones need movement to remain healthy and fully operative.

Therefore when we talk of stress, it is now generally understood to mean unwarranted tension, unrelieved tension, tension which is beyond the effort required for the situation one is in.

The term stress describing a human condition is relatively new and was first coined by Austrian-born Dr. Hans Selye, who said, that stress was simply the rate of wear and tear in the body. However, the term stress is now also used to describe the causes of wear and tear as well as the actual damage done to the body. So stress IS itself, the CAUSE of itself and the RESULT of itself.

We all suffer from stress to some degree. Life is so hectic, we are all so busy, there are so many demands on us, we have so many responsibilities. There is constant noise around us of radio, airplanes, jackhammers, lawnmowers, traffic, dogs barking, children crying. Visually we are trying to cope with the impact of advertising on T.V. and billboards and mentally we have to digest the news on radio and newspapers, most of which seems negative or outright catastrophic. The brain and the mind have to cope with this.

Then there is our "internal noise". In *"Beginning to See"*, A Sujata says: "If we think the noise of traffic is loud, we should go into a quiet room and listen to our minds". Chatter, chatter, chatter... the constant dialogue within continues – our thoughts never still, mulling things over, pleasant or unpleasant. Is it a miracle if we crack up?

Radio, television and popular magazines tell us, that we have to be super mums (or our children will grow up with all kinds of complexes), super wives (or our husbands will tire of us), super lovers (we have to experience orgasms every time we make love or there is something wrong with us), super hostesses (else how is our man going to get his promotion?), super conversationalists (read anything and everything, so our husbands and teen-age children won't consider us dull). Besides this, it is desirable to have a career of our own or, failing this, study for a degree, be involved in sculpting, painting or acquiring other skills to increase our "usefulness." Otherwise we are told that we are vegetating and labelled a cucumber, a cabbage or any other kind of vegetable.

And if you think the female parent is worse off than the male variety, listen to his plight! He has to be a super dad (for the same reason as the super mum), a super husband (same reason as super wives only reverse! Many women now desert their families), super lovers (remember those orgasms? If we don't have them, we can blame his technique or lack of it!), super conversationalists (same reason as above).

Besides this he has to hold down a responsible job in order to be able to meet the mortgage payments on the house and to have ready cash for a host of necessary and unnecessary items. In his job, he has to compete daily with younger, often better educated men who are eager to step into his shoes. Add to both female and male the worries of bringing up a family and the up-keep of a home and you have the stresses and strains of "normal every-day parents" in a nutshell.

Single parents carry an even heavier load as the roles of bread-winner and home-maker have to be combined in the one person without the relief of shared responsibility.

Single people have some of the difficulties mentioned above (they can choose themselves which ones!), as well as such things as coming home to an emply home or flat, nobody to discuss the experiences of the day with, always having to make decisions on their own, no one to lean on, no shoulder to cry on.

So most people are already carrying a heavy load physically and mentally. If this is exacerbated by an unhealthy life style and added stress of, for instance, unharmonious family life, it is little wonder that we find it impossible to cope. We begin to show signs of this in insomnia, migraine head-aches, obesity, constipation, feelings of lethargy and depression, feeling old, feeling restless, not being able to settle down to anything.

We try to combat this by smoking, drinking alcohol, consuming large quantities of sugar and black coffee, taking sleeping tablets, tranquilisers, barbiturates, laxatives, using soft and/or hard drugs.

Of course in pursueing this line of action we only make matters worse. We end up becoming addicted to the so-called remedies and will require an ever-increasing dosage of them to satisfy our needs.

This can lead to consequences such as lung cancer and emphysema of the lungs (smoking), breakdown of the liver (alcohol), breakdown of the kidneys (aspirin and headache powders), sensations of extreme "lows" (sugar and coffee), as well as a general feeling of lack of energy through the malfunctioning of our respiratory and circulatory systems. Our whole metabolism is out of kelter.

Depression worsens, especially through the feeling, that we are no longer in control, no longer our own master, that we are dependent on something outside ourselves, that we are indeed slaves. We have created our own cages!

How true the following poem is, written by an un-known prisoner:

I am caught in a cage I built myself,
Caught by cops I create each day.
Condemned by judges, who preside in me;
Dragged to my cell by my own two arms.
Jail and jailer all in one -
Imprisoned by myself alone
In the circle of self I call my own
Encircled by circles, all my own.

ARE WE GOING TO UNLOCK OUR CAGE AND WALK OUT?

Visit any psychiatric institution and observe how nearly all patients smoke and drink numerous cups of coffee. Many walk around with cigarettes and lighters in their hands as if these constitute the proverbial security blanket.

You may say, that I am painting a very bleak picture and perhaps it does appear as such but these phenomena are all too frequently apparent. Many of us know in our immediate circle of family or friends the person who smokes too much, the businessman on liquid lunches, the housewife with her sherry or headache powders, the young person using drugs, not to mention the large number of unhappy

Before you jump, read the chapter
"Not too much distress about stress"

people who are forever on a diet and never able to stick to it, because they are addicted to the wrong kind of food.

Observe people in the street: a familiar sight is hunched shoulders, clenched fists, tight jaws and foreheads full of frowns. Their faces reflect their inner anxieties. They walk around as if looking for their lost cat.

Have a good look at yourself. Does this description fit you? Are you too "looking for your lost cat"?

It is so unnecessary! Life can be such JOY! Try to stop today – tomorrow never comes.

Remember, today was yesterday's tomorrow and will be tomorrow's yesterday. We so often regret or pine for the past and fear the future, ignoring the "now".

There is a theory proposing that time is not linear, but all-embracing – that all time is always present; that there is no past or future. Nothing **has** happened, but events keep on happening and we link into them as they **happen.**

Therefore, yesterday was NOW, today is NOW, tomorrow will be NOW. No past, no future – NOW. Live it! BE HERE NOW!

Learn to relax. Relaxing is an art which has to be learned. However, to **learn** to relax we must **want** to relax. Letting go is not easy – we like to think that we are in control. Yet, by letting go, we will achieve just that. Once we accept this principle, letting go follows naturally.

Relaxing goes hand in hand with the restoration of the natural breath. People who are ill, who are unwell or who feel they have lost control over their lives, nearly always suffer from some form of impaired breathing. As explained in the chapter on breathing, they either over or under breathe. Both methods will become more and more habitual and enforce the feeling of un-wellness.

Relaxation is traditionally performed lying flat on the back on a firm surface i.e. the floor. However, this can equally successfully be done lying in bed or while sitting in a chair, albeit with a little more preparation.

Although the sitting position as well as the one lying down has been discussed in the chapter on breathing, it does no harm to repeat the instructions at this juncture.

When seated in a chair, make sure that the spine can be held comfortably erect – place a small cushion in the back if needed – the head should be in line with the spine, feel as if the head is balancing on top of the neck. The shoulders are low and relaxed, the hands are in the lap, the palms up, lying one in the other. Do not intertwine the fingers, restricting blood supply to the fingers. A cushion may be placed in the lap to facilitate comfort for the elbows and shoulders. The feet should be firmly planted on the floor and a footstool may be needed to make the legs feel at ease. The eyes are closed. Experiment with the position to make it as comfortable as possible.

Lying down on the back, the body is in a straight line, the head aligned with the spine, the chin toward the chest. The shoulders should be low and relaxed toward the floor, the palms of the hands turned up. The feet twelve to eighteen inches apart, feet turned outward. (See part 3.)

If it is uncomfortable to lie flat on the back because of low back trouble, place a pillow under the bent knees, rather than placing a small cushion under the lumbar. I feel that this will only increase the tendency of over-arching the lower area of the spine, whereas a pillow under the knees will assist the spine in flattening out.

If there is a tendency for the head to fall back, thereby, putting a strain on the throat, place a small cushion under the back of the head.

Make sure that you are warm enough, using a rug if needed, as during relaxation the body temperature drops through the slowing down of the metabolism as a consequence of the lower rate of respiration and heart beat.

During relaxation you should not fall asleep, the mind should remain alert as the body relaxes. The state of sleep is different from the state of relaxation. When we are asleep we move mentally toward unconsciousness – when we relax, we move toward a higher state of awareness. If you should fall asleep however, do not worry. You will find, that it is a wonderful kind of sleep, which will leave you very refreshed. This is because the body is relaxed, all residual tension removed.

Many people derive very little benefit from the sleep they have. I have heard people say, that they wake up virtually as exhausted as they were when they went to bed. Some people are so tense, that even during sleep they are unable to relax. They grind their teeth all night and wake up with their jaws locked or their hands in tight fists.

If you don't wake up with a sparkle in your eyes, check that your bedroom is well-ventilated. Perhaps you have too many blankets on the bed, becoming too hot during the night. This will adversely affect your sleep, often causing you to dream. Don't go to sleep with a full stomach – try to avoid late heavy meals – these too will do nothing to enhance the quality of your sleep. If all these factors check out all right and you still have trouble falling asleep, try my sighing technique:

Lie in bed and let go of as much tension as you can, making yourself comfortable. Then take a deep breath in through the nose, expanding the ribcage – gently open the mouth and audibly sigh the breath out: aaaaahhhhh. Again, in through the nose – deep breath – out through the mouth sighing: aaaaaahhhhhhhh. Not forcibly pushing the air out:

haaaaaaa, but letting the air flow out sighing: aaaaaa-hhhhhhhhhhh. As you sigh, feel yourself sinking into the mattress, becoming heavier and heavier. In through the nose, deep, deep breath in – out through the mouth sighing: aaaaaaahhhhhh, feeling the tension flow out – out of the finger tips and out of the tips of the toes: aaaaahhhhhh. You will find this will make you fall asleep.

We should become like little children – we should FALL asleep, not GO to sleep. Observe a toddler in his bed: one moment he is wide awake, standing up in bed, playing with his toys, making a noise and perhaps talking to himself. The next moment SILENCE, as he has literally FALLEN asleep, often lying in the midst of or on top of the toys he was playing with.

Something happens on the way to adulthood – adults no longer fall asleep. Instead, many lie in bed tossing and turning, waiting for sleep to come, telling themselves, that if they don't get to sleep soon, they will be a wreck in the morning. (Tell yourself that often enough and you will be!) Have you ever noticed, that sleep is even more elusive on the eve of an important day? It is your tension which keeps you awake. Try my sighing and EXPECT to fall asleep!

If you don't, ask yourself why it is that sleep won't come. Do you have a specific worry? Some problem to solve? In that case, don't force yourself to go to sleep. Even if you were successful, the kind of sleep you would experience, would not be worth much. Instead, **AFTER** the sighing, lie quietly and consider the problem.

First of all establish whether it is indeed your problem and not someone else's. We so badly want to help our loved ones, we are so closely tied to our children, that it often becomes difficult to distinguish between our problem and theirs. If it isn't your problem, **you can turn over and fall asleep.** If you decide, that it is yours, determine whether you can do anything about it. If you can, decide on a course of action and make a firm resolve to set this in motion as soon as is practicable, **then fall asleep.** If it is a problem you cannot change, accept that this is so and make up your mind to try to make the most of what you perceive to be a bad situation. You will find that **you will fall asleep quite easily,** as it is often the worry about something we have not wanted to face properly which keeps us awake. In other words it is fear. Recognizing what the problem is, takes the fear out of the situation and hence the tension which made us lie awake. Also, don't worry too much about the amount of sleep you have. It is the quality of sleep, the relaxed and restoring sleep which matters, not the quantity.

A good way to learn relaxation is by tensing and relaxing every part of the body in turn with total awareness of the tensing and letting go; consciously experiencing "what it feels like to be tense" and consciously experiencing "what it feels like to be relaxed". Once we master the technique of relaxation, this will be no longer necessary as it will become increasingly more simple to let go. However, having consciously experienced the difference between the tense state and the relaxed state, will help us in everyday life, as we will be able to recognise tension before it builds up.

Lying comfortably on the floor or bed or sitting in a chair, pull the small of the back in tightly, tensing the muscles in the stomach – feel the tension – and let go: abdomen is soft and relaxed, small of the back is comfortable. Pull the shoulders back, expand your chest – feel the tension – and let go: chest is soft and relaxed, shoulders low and relaxed. Now become aware of your spine – feel the spine unwind, each vertebra, each disc, soft and relaxed – whole spine, whole torso soft and relaxed.....

Pull your feet tightly toward your head – feel the tension – right up into the hips, and let go: toes dropping outward, ankles soft, calves and knees collapsing into the floor, thighs are heavy – both feet, both legs relaxed..... Make tight fists, tense the muscles in the arms tightly – feel the tension – and let go: hands falling open, the fingers gently curled, wrists soft, forearms and elbows falling into the floor, upper arms and shoulders low and relaxed – both hands, both arms relaxed..... Pull the chin toward the chest – feel the tension – then let the head find a comfortable position. If you can, keep the head in the centre. If you don't find that comfortable, don't worry – you are now relaxing. Swallow and relax your throat – throat and neck relaxed..... Screw you face up tightly – feel the tension around the mouth, the nose, the eyes, into the forehead, into the area of the scalp, around the ears – and let go: feel the facial muscles settle – the cheeks are soft and floppy, the areas around the eyes are soft, no lines, no frowns in the forehead and the skin over the skull is soft and pliable – each hair on your head seems relaxed..... Lick your lips, then leave them slightly apart, don't bite your teeth. Let the lower jaw fall, make it heavy, let it go as the tongue lies relaxed on the floor of the mouth. Whole face, whole head relaxed.....

Then pass your mind back over you body – checking: muscles behind the knees are soft, small of the back is relaxed, no tension between the shoulder blades, no tension around the mouth and the eyes. The eyelids are closed and the eyes are dropping inward. You are not rolling the eyes up – no tension – just let them fall into the skull. You are inward-looking, unconcerned with anything external. All you want to do is RELAX, **Whole body is soft – whole body is relaxed – whole body is motionless.....**

Inhale deeply through the nose expanding the ribcage as in energising breathing and, opening the mouth softly, sigh the breath out. Take another breath in again only when you feel the need to do so. The inhalation is deep and full, the exhalation is complete – no air left. However **do not force the air out** – that would be defeating the purpose! Feel all the tension, the worries, fatigue, the rushing and hurrying of the day flow away from you as you sigh. In through the nose, out through the mouth sighing – letting go with each sigh.....

When you feel soft and relaxed, gently close the mouth and continue breathing through the nose – deeply and slowly without too much effort involved, but a conscious inhalation and exhalation, expanding and contracting the rib-cage. During the first stage of relaxation there is body awareness and energising breathing. During the later stages of relaxation body consciousness "falls away", the breath becomes relaxed as we are then only concerned with the mind.

Know, that with each inhalation Life Force, Cosmic Energy, enters the body – this is retained by the body – on the exhalation, only the air leaves the body. See the Life Force as a golden energy stream or as a stream of bright white energy if you can't visualise colours. If visualising is difficult for you, try to experience the Life Force as a stream of warmth.

Breathing in: energy, health, vitality, strength – Breathing out: aches, pains, discomforts, stiffness, weakness, Do this for several breaths, mentally repeating the above to yourself. See the Life Force replace all the negativity on the physical level. Remember, we are working with a REAL FORCE! Visualisation is a very powerful tool and is more and more widely used to combat serious illnesses.

Continue with Inhaling: peace, tranquility, harmony – Exhaling: tension, worries, agitation. Inhaling: calmness, peace, love – Exhaling: stress, hate, jealousy, resentment. Repeat this for several more breaths.....

Then inhaling: positive thought – Exhaling: release all negative thought. Repeat this several times. Always consciously replacing a negative thought with a positive one. Inhaling: positive attitude – Exhaling: negative attitude. Inhaling: "I can" – Exhaling: "I can't". Not "I will", which indicates a clenched fist and hence tension, but "I can", which is the open hand, indicating confidence and trust. Inhale: "I can"..... Exhale: "I can't".....

Then let go of the energising breath – you are no longer involved with your breathing. The ribcage becomes still and the abdomen will gently rise and fall with the relaxed breath. No conscious effort involved – no thought involved. Check that your body is still relaxed. If you find tension anywhere, do not move, but let go of that tension. Feel as if you are melting....., the whole body dissolving..... and send your mind away from where you are to a place of peace, your special retreat..... a place which is private, you don't discuss it with others....., a place where you feel at home....., it may be real or imaginary..... the main thing is that you feel happy there..... It is a haven in a busy, noisy world – it is like balm for the soul... Feel it – experience it..... Let the serenity and tranquility of the place saturate your whole being.....

Now let the mind become still..... no images..... no pictures..... The eyes are inwardly directed..... no strain in the area of the eyes just let yourself go..... Then feel as if there is a second set of eyelids below the ones that are already closed – and feel them drop-shut.....

If you find it difficult..... if thoughts keep intruding..... Imagine, that you are sitting by a pond..... you have just dropped a pebble into the water..... see the ever-widening ripples..... then concentrate on the still centre..... the still centre.....

This pond is not unlike your mind with its thoughts... ripple, ripple, ripple... We are getting in touch with our still centre...

Coming out of your relaxation, take your time – do not hurry getting up – let the mind and body become adjusted to movement again. Return your mind to your body and begin wriggling your toes, being aware of each movement. Where for a while there was little or no body awareness, Now you become most aware of it. Feel how it moves. Rotate the ankles, bend the knees, pulling the small of the back into the floor or the chair and letting go again; shrugging the shoulders, making fists and bending the elbows, then stretching the arms and hands up to the ceiling, roll from side to side. Finally roll onto the right side of the body and curl up for a few moments before sitting up.

It is important to get up slowly after a relaxation session. As mentioned before, during deep relaxation the metabolism slows down and the body temperature drops due to slower breathing and heart rate. Rising quickly might make you dizzy, causing you to fall.

If you should have to get up quickly for something important (the doorbell rings and you hope that it might be a representative of Lotto with the message that you have won a million dollars!), get onto hands and knees and crawl to your destination. Do stand up though before you open the door – your caller (most likely not the one you hoped it would be) might think that you are suffering an identity crisis, imagining yourself to be the family pet!

Perhaps you could learn the relaxation by heart or tape it. An idea might be to have someone read it to you or perhaps you could join up with some friends and relax together. This might prove to be a real treat!

If you are feeling inadequate, if you have feelings of "I can't" about most things; when as children we answered a directive of our mother with: "I can't do that!", she would reply: "Cannot lies at the cemetery – those people no longer can!" "You should at least try!" Perhaps my mother was a natural Yogi, I don't know. She was certainly very positive – I don't think I ever saw her depressed. Perhaps you would like to consider the advice of my mother next time you hear yourself say "I can't".

All my students know my mother – now that I have told you about her, you know her a little too. I find it exciting to think, that she does not only live on through her seven children and other people she touched during her lifetime, but also through the numerous people I have reached. I think she would like that.

How we see things, how we experience life, often depends entirely on our state of mind. As Kahlil Gibran writes: "The appearance of things changes according to the emotions, and thus we see magic and beauty in them, while the magic and beauty are really in ourselves". (from K.G.s book *"Broken Wings"* mentioned in the 2nd Treasury of K.G.) So if instead there are darkness and negativity in us, we will see darkness and negativity in whatever we are looking at.

Remember, we are all unique – we all have our special talents. Do not compare yourself or your situation with others; we can never fully appreciate other people's worries and situations. Who knows, they may be comparing themselves unfavourably with you! Do not get bogged down with the things you **cannot** do, concentrate instead on the things you **can,** even if it is only one – and build on that.

Don't be depressed about your limitations. We are all limited to some degree – some more obviously and visibly than others – some of us hide it better! Consider, that they do not have to REMAIN your limitations – YOU ARE NOT SET IN CONCRETE!

Picture what you perceive as your limitations – see them as a barrier of encircling walls positioned around you – you are in the centre. The smaller you envisage the circle to be, the more towering your so-called limitations will seem and the more chance there is, that they will collapse upon you and bury you.

Instead, with total trust and knowing that it is possible, visualise, that you are gently pushing against the barriers from the inside – enlarging the circle, widening it – stretching it little by little.

Don't think "I will", which is the force-reaction, generating more stress; think "I can", which is the relaxed way of building confidence in yourself – enlarging the circle so wide, that the sunlight of a tranquil mind will reach you from all sides - dissolving the earlier perceived barriers like mirages.

Everything seems simple in nature..... until we try to find out what makes one blade of grass grow.

CHAPTER 6

MAN'S EASIEST ROAD TO SUICIDE

Why is it, that we begin to feel physically unwell when we are depressed? Why is it, that mind and body seem to work in tandem? When we are feeling well, our thinking is positive – when we are feeling unwell, our thinking is negative. Or is it when our thinking is positive we are feeling well – when our thinking is negative we are feeling unwell.

Which comes first, the thought or the physical state? In other words does the way we think influence the body or does the body influence the way we think? Does the emotional/mental "us" influence the physical "us", or is it the other way round?

Science seems to begin to accept the fact, that it is the mind, which to a large degree is responsible for our physical condition. It is more than positive thinking, it is our whole approach to life.

Hence the terms "stress" and "relaxation response" were invented for states of the body, which are a direct result of the influence of the mind.

It is an absolute miracle, that the Yogis knew this already many centuries ago (some say even before the Christian era). They did not have the tools and equipment of the twentieth century to prove that they were correct, all they had was their intuitive knowledge.

The Yogis knew the importance of a balanced hormonal flow. They appreciated that the food we eat influences not only the body, but also the mind. They realised that relaxation and meditation are beneficial for the mental state, and directly influence the physical state of the person. They taught about the function of the pituitary, the pineal and the thymus glands (although they did not have a name for them). They acknowledged that a healthy and well-functioning body will make it easier to be peaceful – that we need stillness in order to be a whole person. And finally, they knew that respiration is the most important function of the body – that the breath is the link between the physical and the mental/emotional/spiritual part of the person. All this was **intuitive knowledge!**

Considering this, we haven't really progressed a great deal. We have largely lost our intuition and even if we had any, the only knowledge which is acceptable in our "high tech" age is knowledge which can be proven to be correct. This century says, that nothing is true unless it can be scientifically proven to be so – Yoga says, that all is true, all is possible, until it is proven not to be.

Researchers into illness, working with electronic equipment such as biofeedback machines tell us that there is such a thing as the "fight and flight syndrome", something which stood us in good stead in the time of the cave man, when we suddenly could be confronted by a large wild animal. This body reaction gives us instant energy beyond our every-day capacity through the injection of adrenalin into the body system. The heart rate increases, blood pressure rises, the circulation becomes more rapid, there is increased muscle tension, the mind focusses intently and the breathing rate alters to be able to deal with this emergency. All this to give the cave man the wherewithal either to stay and fight the animal or to leg it!! When the emergency was resolved, the cave man went "Aaaaaah-hhhhh" and rested with his cave woman in their cave for a while in the knowledge of a job well done.

Stop fooling around Fred!
You are stressing the dragon...

This is now called the "relaxation response" and accepted to be exactly what we need after an adventure, which triggered off such an intense body reaction.

Although we know intellectually, that we are no longer cave men, that we no longer need this physical reaction as it is highly unlikely that we will encounter a wild beast on the way to work, emotionally we react in the same wav to our twentieth century stressors as our predecessors did to theirs.

The body does not differentiate whether the response is appropriate under the circumstances or not – it reacts to our signals. And hence, each time we are irritated, angry, upset – in the new term "stressed" – we go through the whole body response as if we were indeed facing this wild creature.

What makes this body response so damaging is the multitude of stressful situations with which modern life presents us, coupled with the fact that most of us have lost the art of relaxation, which is the proper antidote for this physical state of emergency. There is nothing wrong with stress. In fact, we need it for proper functioning – we could not do without it. It is the **unrelieved** stress, which is detrimental to our state of well-being. We need to be able to react to our signals of danger; short-term they can be life-saving. It is our reaction to our every-day irritations which is inappropriate. We go "over the top".

It has now been documented that when this response to every-day life situations becomes habitual, the body is in a constant state of emergency or stress. This not only triggers off the physical consequences mentioned above – there is more! We learn, that it is not just the adrenal glands working overtime producing cortisols as well as adrenalin, but that most of the endocrine glands join in the fray. It is said that we effectively poison our own bodies, that some people even become addicted to their own body substances!

And yet, to me this does not seem to be the whole story. It is documented (evidenced during autopsy), that there are many people with advanced malignant tumors, or with considerable damage to the myelin sheath around the nerve fibres of the brain and spinal cord, who had no signs, either of cancer or of multiple sclerosis prior to their deaths.

So what is it, that makes one person succumb to an illness, while another leads the life of a totally healthy individual?

Whereas it is intellectually satisfying to know the current scientific position on well-being and illness, it must be remembered, that present opinion may change in the future when other evidence becomes available. It has happened in the past; a theory which seemed totally acceptable one moment, was thrown out the next and replaced by a more plausible one. We all know from personal experience or from anecdotal evidence, that an operation or other medical treatment which was deemed essential and life-saving one time, was "shoulder-shrugged" a few years later.....

I am convinced, that the Yogis had the answer and that their theories are as valid today as they were when they were first propounded. Scientific evidence is only interesting (head stuff), it is not vital. Vital is, that we understand it with our hearts on an intuitive level. The intrinsic knowledge is there – all we have to do is tune into it – become aware – still.....

We'll have to go back to the Yoga philosophy and its theory that the breath is the source of life. Howard Kent in his book "Yoga for Handicapped People", tells us on page 60, how he fractured his zygomatic arch (part of the cheek bone). When offered an operation, he refused. However, when he used an electronic machine which indicates electric receptivity of the body's tissue fluid, which in turn largely depends on the person's state of health, it was found that the part which was fractured and the area around it, was way below normal. All Howard then did, was sit down quietly for five minutes and practise the energising breath, visualising the energy flowing into the damaged area. The next electronic reading proved that this had indeed happened and the reading was quite normal. However, a further reading indicated that this energy was depleted quite quickly. From this Howard deduced that, if he paid more attention than usual to his breathing and used the visualising technique, he could effectively influence the healing of his injured body part.

The yogis had no electronic instruments, no X-ray machines, no other diagnostic tools. They only talked about respiration and about Life Force - Prana. And this is where I feel the answer lies. We have to go back to our intuition – develop that as much as we can – get in touch with the real issues – get in touch with ourselves.

Whether we have cancer or only the common cold, whether we have multiple sclerosis or just feel off-colour, whether we have anxiety or are plagued by acne, IT IS ALL THE SAME! We are lacking in Life Force!

When we are tense or anxious, we create tension in certain body areas sometimes resulting in tightness in the throat, head-aches, butterflies in the stomach, pains in the chest, cramps in the abdomen often causing us to go to the toilet much more frequently than normal, involuntary muscle tremors and spasms, cold hands and feet – we have all experienced this.

At such a time it would be interesting to check the way we breathe. Odds are that we are hyper ventilating, breathing rapidly and shallowly. It is very difficult to breathe deeply, using expansion and contraction of the ribcage, when there is discomfort and pain. And yet, **this is exactly what we need to do!**

It is the breath, which links us into the Life Force – it is the Life Force, which has the healing properties. Without correct breathing, the body becomes starved of nutrition and this is what happens when we are tense and our breathing is affected. On a physical level the blood supply to the injured area is impeded – on a more subtle level we also close the energy channels. We set up "road closed" signs, effectively starving certain limbs or organs of nutrition and of vital energy, the Life Force.

And yet, as stated before, it is the respiration which puts us in charge. We do not have to feel like victims. We are not under attack from the outside – we are doing it ourselves!

I have noticed, that a large percentage of our society expects to be ill or to become ill. Nobody shows surprise at any illness we develop, yet very frequently surprise is expressed at recovery from an illness.

If someone told you that he or she needed surgery to have a malignant tumor removed, would you feel the urge to ask that person: "How did you grow it?" Would it enter your mind, that growing something is a mystery – that no one has the answer yet as to what spark ignites the growth process? And yet, you would certainly feel compelled to ask: "How did you do it?", if after some months you were told that instead of surgery, this person had meditated several hours each day and now X-rays indicated that the tumor had completely disappeared. You might even (silently or aloud) want to proclaim it a miracle.

Did the thought ever cross your mind that growing something is as much a miracle – nay, that it is a mystery? If it were not a mystery, medical science would have the cure for cancer. Knowing how something originates, would supply the answer for the method to stop that growth from occurring.

We as a society seem **disease** oriented – accepting and expecting illness. We must become **wellness** oriented – accepting **that** as the norm. If we can accept that we can grow tumors, divide cells and grow a multitude of them, then we must learn to accept that we can "un-grow" them – that we have the power to let the tumors disappear by making those cells behave normally.

We should realise, that when we are diagnosed to have an "incurable, degenerative disease", this only means the following:
Incurable – a cure has not been found yet;
Degenerative – from observation and historical evidence the physical health of the person afflicted appears to deteriorate.

How can an honest diagnosis be made as to whether a disease is degenerative, if one does not know what the illness is? (remember "incurable"?) Why then should we accept this to be the situation for the rest of our lives? Life is fluid – we are constantly changing, constantly moving, nothing is ever totally still.

Why could not our state of health change for the better instead of for the worse? Could it not be that what is destroyed within the body can also be regenerated, created within the body? When a lizard breaks off part of its tail, it has the ability to regrow it. Why then could we not be our own healer? Are we less than a lizard?

Don't label yourself: "I am a diabetic", "an asthmatic", "a cancer or stroke victim", "an M.S. sufferer". YOU ARE WHO YOU ARE – the SAME PERSON YOU WERE BEFORE YOU BECAME ILL. You are indisposed now, but that does no have to remain like that. You are not set in concrete!

Especially the terms "victim" and "sufferer" indicate a helplessness on the part of the person afflicted, which implies that help, if any, will have to come from others.

If a label has to be put on a sick person, "patient" is a much better term. It implies, that if one is patient, one can become better. PATIENCE is involved in the healing process. That and TRUST and the KNOWLEDGE, that healing is POSSIBLE!

During illness, do not only identify with the body. We are more than the body – we are body, mind and spirit. See illness as a lesson to learn. We learn many things when we are sick. We learn about ourselves – how patient we are, what expectations we have of ourselves and of others, what our priorities are, how fixed our ideas are as to how certain things need to be done, what our level of endurance to pain is, whether our sense of humour is as well developed as we thought it was, how soon we become despondent, desperate even and get into a panic state, whether we are courageous enough to look the situation squarely in the face or would rather sweep it under the carpet, pretending it is not happening to us. How well are we coping?.

It is important not to panic. Observe a sick animal – it becomes extremely quiet, sits still, eats little, encouraging energy flow. People do the exact opposite – running from this healer to that healer, trying this method then another, wasting precious energy through tension and depression. BE STILL and contemplate what it is you need to do, what it is you want, what degree of health you need to live effectively – then set about getting well. Keep the image of how you would like to be clearly before your mind's eye. Set about restoring the natural breathing pattern and visualise the Life Force, on entering the body, to flow into the affected body part(s). Do this as often as you can.

As there is substantial documentation of the detrimental effects of the "fight or flight syndrome" on the body, so there is an equal amount of evidence of the beneficial effects of the "relaxation response".

It is accepted that exercise and meditation release endorphins (pituitary proteins) in the body. It is thought that they make their presence felt by activating the immune system and by relaxing the adrenal glands. It has been found, that during deep relaxation restricted respiratory passages have widened (asthmatics), that there is less need for insulin for someone with diabetes. A lowering of blood pressure and cholesterol levels have been registered, the heart rate slows down, circulation normalises, the rate and depth of breathing become stable and muscle tension returns to a normal level. This only happens during deep relaxation and meditation, not when we are watching T.V. or quietly reading a book, relaxed as we might feel then.

What constitutes stress? There is no easy answer to that question. An incident which causes stress to one person may be a laugh to someone else and vice versa. It is thought, that it is not so much the actual happening which causes the damage, but our reaction to that happening. If our reaction is inappropriate for the occasion, if there are too many of such instances, if we are unaware, that this is in fact happening to us, the results of the stress reaction can become chronic, resulting in feelings of uneasiness. We will experience feelings of dis-ease, resulting in disease.

It is important to all of us, the already-sick-person and the still-well-person, to ask ourselves: "How are we coping?" "Are we as well as we believe we are?" – Let us look at the way we breathe. Are we using our ribcages? Do we breathe deeply and slowly under most circumstances? If the answer is "no", obviously we are already affected by the stress we are under but there is still time to adopt a different way of coping. On the other hand, let us ask ourselves: "Are we as sick as we believe we are?" Again let us look at the way we breathe. If we are sick, odds are, that our breathing is impaired.

This chapter would not be complete if the matter of diet were not raised. Many books have been written on the subject by people much better qualified than I and so I shall not be so presumptuous as to tell you what is good for you and what is not.

Whenever the subject of a healthy diet is raised, we hear comments like: "I enjoy my ice cream, cakes, porkchops, chocolates… without them life is not worth much!" Another argument is: "We all have to die of something, I want to enjoy myself while I am here." But this is just the point! Is only food, which is detrimental to the body enjoyable? How long does that enjoyment last – ten minutes? Half an hour? People may even enjoy it in retrospect, remembering it – or in anticipation, while preparing it or expecting it on the table, thereby extending the duration of their enjoyment. However, that time is still relatively short, if one considers that they will have to live with the consequences of that food for the rest of their lives.

Of course we all have to die sometime of something, that should not worry us unduly. What should concern us is the quality of life and the kind of death we'll experience. In fact, we should not even be concerned about the length of our life, but about the length of our youth, wanting to extend the creative years of our life.

Most people are affected by the wrong diet. Some are not even aware of it, rationalising their condition with remarks such as, "I am not eighteen any longer", "I am getting old", "I am not as young as I used to be".

Don't expect to creak after your fortieth birthday! Don't write yourself off! Your body does not have to break down so quickly. Why should the adult body be no longer a thing of beauty?

One of the reasons we enjoy going to the Ballet is seeing beautiful bodies making music visible. Of course, they are trained bodies, not to be compared with ours, non-artists, slogging away at our daily endeavours. But is this necessarily so? Why shouldn't we be able to look after our bodies with equal care and be beautiful performers in the ballet of life?

The body should move with ease and grace – it should become an instrument with which to express the Joy of Being Alive. In that case the body would not only be a joy for the person inside it, but also for the beholder.

Of course, blaming all ailments on a faulty diet is over-simplifying matters. It is logical though, that in order to function properly, the body needs energy brought about through correct breathing as well as that supplied by proper nutrition.

Those of us cooking for a family carry an awesome responsibility. We are not only feeding the next generation but also instilling eating habits in them. We are creatures of habit – habits are hard to break. Many obese persons have been heard to blame their mothers for putting cakes and soft drinks in their lunch boxes and offering the same fare as a snack after school. Considering this: don't insist that children eat everything on their plates – they know when they have had enough. However, don't offer them food in between meals if they did not finish the previous meal. Also, don't give them sweets as a reward for good behaviour.

This does not mean, that we have to become fanatic. Let there be all the party food they want on special occasions – that way, these will become special occasions which will stand out in the child's memory. But don't let party food become every-day fare.

Perhaps you would like to look into vegetarianism. There seems evidence to support the theory, that people, who abstain from meat, are not as prone to contract the twentieth century sicknesses as those for whom meat is on the daily menu.

Introduce changes in the family diet gradually. It is no use upsetting everybody. Talk it over – explain the reasons why you feel a change may be beneficial. You need their enthusiasm and co-operation. Introduce first one meatless day per week. This will give you an opportunity to change your way of approaching a menu too. Do it slowly, that way there is no shock to either body or mind. Easy does it!

Look at the window sill of the kitchen or in the bathroom cabinet of middle-aged or older people. Looking at all the little bottles, it would seem that they need quite a few pills and potions to help them through each day. And these are usually prescribed drugs. Some of the chemicals introduced into the body by those medicines have been known to trigger off side-effects, starting a chain reaction of other complaints. The medical profession is becoming increasingly more aware of this.

There is now a word for becoming sick through medication: iatrogenic – or doctor induced illness. In a survey carried out at St. Bartholomew's Hospital, London, 12½ percent, or one in eight, of the patients was in this category. This was as a result of accepted forms of treatment and did not include doctors' mistakes.

Some adults are to be pitied – they behave like potential suicides! Australia has the dubious honour of being high on the list of countries with regard to consumption of prescribed and over-the-counter drugs as well as of alcohol, while the incidence of cigarette smoking seems to be on the increase among the younger folk and women.

If we are in a position of authority, of role models for the young; parents, teachers, politicians, we will have to consider how our behaviour influences the child and young adult. No use expecting them to refrain from using negative substances if we can't or won't do this ourselves. Swami Sarasvati once said: "We have to be the medium of our own message". In other words: "Deeds speak louder than words" or "Let our practice be our preacher!"

If a drug came on the market purporting to promote eternal youth, we would do anything, pay any amount to obtain this potion. Yet it seems impossible for us to heed the warnings which are coming thick and fast, telling us, that the effects of old-age (breakdown of the body system) are brought forward by our destructive life style. It seems too difficult to take some care, to be disciplined.

We let the body become like a spoilt child – giving it what it wants, not what it needs. It wants tobacco, alcohol, sugar, salt... The mind, like a weak parent lets the body get away with it. Instead of being our strongest part, it becomes our weakest, rationalising its weakness by saying: "I know I shouldn't..." "I don't usually do this, eat that..." "just this once..."

And yet the mind can be so powerful! Some people confuse the mind with the brain. The brain is the grey matter, which is inside the skull – the brain is the tool of the mind, the thought. It has been found, that thought precedes action – that thought sparks off electrical impulses in the relevant brain area before action can occur.

The mind is all-pervasive – it cannot be contained. It can go where it wants to go, be where it wants to be – it is without bounds. While the body is in one place, the mind can travel anywhere in a split second. So let us realise that we as a person are contained within the mind and that hence its influence can be tremendous.

Those who want to reduce weight should consider the following: It takes only one firm resolve to lose weight. Only when your mind is made up, when you are really serious about losing those extra kilos, will it begin to happen. In that frame of mind you will not find it too difficult to change your diet, or to eat a little less. You will only need this resolve during the first week or so. Once you begin to shed those pounds, the weight loss itself will be an incentive.

In that situation you will receive great support from your daily Yoga practice. The discipline of it will permeate your whole lifestyle. We are wasting so much precious time looking after a body, which is breaking down all over the place. Something that breaks down asks for attention – something that functions well can be forgotten.

The daily Yoga practice will accelerate your metabolism through the influence of the asanas and movements on the digestive, circulatory and eliminative systems, as well as stimulate the endocrinal glandular system. There are no "do's" and "don'ts" in Yoga. Start practising and you will find that your physical, mental and emotional demands will change.

We are not only what we eat. We are also what we hear, see, say, what we read, whom we associate with. As food has to be digested by the body, so has that which enters our senses to be digested by the mind. Think about it! What we see on T.V., what we hear on the radio, the books we read, all become mental images. Negative images are very hard to get rid of – they lie as heavily on the mind as the wrong food can lie on the stomach. So, too, can people we associate with have a great influence on us. We have to learn to discriminate – to become aware people.

If we are sick, let us ask ourselves two questions before we do anything else:
"Do I really want to get better?"
"Do I need this illness?"

Usually the first reaction is: "Of course, I want to get better" and "No, of course I do not need this illness." Some people become angry; some feel the questions imply that they could get well if only they really wanted to be well. This is too simple. However, answering those questions requires an enormous amount of honesty with ourselves and unless we have the answer to those questions firmly in our minds, there will be no improvement in our health.

Often getting better may involve a tremendous effort and we may not deem this worth our while. Sometimes, on reflection, we may realise that although we are missing out on many aspects of life through being ill, the overall quality of life has improved.

There is more time for listening and contemplation, the rushing and hurrying is no longer expected of us, we are no longer involved in taking difficult decisions, there is more meaningful contact with those around us.

Improved health may result in losing a pension or other financial assistance and having to work for a living, the prospect of which can be exciting, but also very daunting after many years of illness.

Sometimes wives may consider the illness a way of keeping their husbands by their sides – husbands their wives. An endless list of possibilities; a true Pandora's box!

Kahlil Gibran, says the following on this subject, putting it so much more eloquently than I:

> *"I have found pleasure in being ill. This pleasure differs with its effects from any other pleasure. I have found a sort of tranquility that makes me love illness. The sick man is safe from people's strife, demands, dates and appointments, excess of talking and ringing of telephones... I have found another kind of enjoyment through illness which is more important and unmeasureable. I have found, that I am closer to abstract things in*

my sickness than in health. When I lay my head and close my eyes and lose myself to the world, I find myself flying like a bird over serene valleys and forests, wrapped in a gentle veil. I see myself close to those whom my heart has loved, calling and talking to them, but without anger and with the same feelings they feel and the same thoughts they think. They lay their hands now and then upon my forehead to bless me."

(from Kahlil Gibran *"A Self Portrait"* – taken from second Treasury of Kahlil Gibran).

If you have decided that you want to get better, or if you feel that it is high time you did something positive about the way you react to whatever it is life dishes up to you, please consider seriously taking up relaxation and/or meditation. You will not regret it.

It is easier to relax after physical movement has released the residual tension in the body. When the body is relaxed, it is most receptive to healing. Yoga is the ideal type of exercise for everyone, well or not-so-well. All postures and movements can be tailored and adapted to the requirements of the individual.

Yoga gives us courage – strengthens our resolve – teaches us the correct way of breathing – increases our discipline. It gives us a clear choice: Are we going to aim at Peace of Mind or are we going to settle for Conflict? Yoga gives us the strength to face ourselves and to see ourselves as we truly are. It makes us accept the past, cope with the present and plan for the future with confidence and trust.

Yoga makes us assess our relationships – our relationship with ourselves and our relationships with others. Christ has said: "Love thy neighbour as thyself". Implied in this is that we should love ourselves – be at ease, at peace with ourselves. How else is this command going to benefit our neighbour? Loving ourselves is the pure level of acceptance of **what is.** Wanting to put ourselves down, not liking our own excellence is negative.

Yoga teaches us Ahimsa, a Sanskrit word, which translates as non-violence: It asks: what am I doing to promote non-violence in the world – what am I doing to promote non-violence in my country, my city, my family? What am I doing to promote non-violence to myself?

Yoga also teaches Santosha, another Sanskrit word, which translates as contentment. Contentment with our place in life – contentment with who we are and what we are. Contentment with our condition: BE HERE NOW – I AM THAT. I am part of the universe, part of all there is, part of creation. It teaches us to live within this concept in today's world.

CHAPTER 7

ME MEDITATING? YOU MUST BE KIDDING!

This was my reaction when I was asked whether I practised meditation. This is many years ago now and was mainly due to ignorance of course. I had no idea what meditation was and the word conjured up images of strange Eastern practices. I feel I was not alone in this and even today it is not unusual to receive an answer like mine. Why is this so? We read in the Bible, that Jesus went into the desert to meditate and certainly meditative practices have been an integral part of religious life for nuns and monks through the ages.

Still one encounters people who are opposed to it on religious grounds, having obviously misunderstood what meditation is, while there are many people, who seem to shy away from it – appearing almost afraid to discuss it.

Much has been written about meditation in newspapers and magazines since I was asked the question and today there is a better understanding of how meditation can influence both mind and body.

What is meditation?
Meditation is "profound thinking – pondering", according to Webster, Meditation is "plan mentally – design, exercise the mind in contemplation", according to the concise Oxford dictionary.

One dictionary says meditation is intensive thinking, while yet another one states meditation is absence of thought. No wonder there is such confusion!

There are many definitions of meditation. Here are a few of them:

Meditation is an inward journey, a homecoming as if in a safe harbour.

Meditation is a beam of perceiving consciousness when all is revealed.

Meditation transcends the limitations of the intellect. A new vantage point is acquired. We can't see around corners, however standing on the roof we can. (Michael Volin)

In meditation we come to something we possessed as children; wisdom and innocence.

In meditation the imperceivable is perceived, the impossible becomes possible.

In meditation we can experience our inner resources. Within us is the same Divine Power that created the universe. (Judith Stalls, taken from International Light magazine)

The Buddha says: Without knowledge/awareness, there is no meditation. Without meditation, there is no knowledge. And he who has both knowledge and meditation is near to reality.

In prayer I talk, God listens – in meditation God talks, I listen.

Meditation is the process whereby one creates a break between the physical and the mental/spiritual. (Howard Kent)

Meditation is moving from the physical plane into inner space – the dwelling place of the soul.

The list is endless – the definitions many.

To me meditation is getting in touch with the great stillness which is within all of us. Some of us have buried it so deeply, that we are wondering whether it exists at all. It is imperative for our mental and physical health that we are in touch with this stillness at least once a day.

The best way to remove the mystery is to experience meditation. I suppose one has to be ready for it. This does not depend on age or sex or on how long one has been practising Yoga. However I believe, that there are a few pre-requisites such as:

1.– Being able to sit still for a certain amount of time – if the body is not still, we are creating our own disturbances.
   The traditional Yoga position for meditation is sitting crosslegged. The reason for this is that, in this position, the buttocks, thighs, knees and lower part of the legs form a triangle, creating a stable platform on which to rest the top part of the body. This also makes it easier to keep the spine erect, which is **essential** for effective meditation. However, any sitting position is suitable as long as the spine is aligned.
2.– A certain maturity – although children meditate quite effectively. It is obvious, that for a person whose concentration span is short, meditation will present more difficulties. However, meditation will increase the concentration span and accelerate the maturing process of the mind.
3.– A genuine desire to get to know oneself.
   One must be motivated to meditate – to sit still for at least twenty minutes each day requires a discipline and a goal.

To be able to come to true meditation, we have to learn to relax, to be motionless, to concentrate, to contemplate and to disgard the body while remaining aware of it. This seems a tall order and it is, but it is an exciting path!

Meditation has been called a journey inwards. By the same token it could be called a journey out of oneself – away from the eternal internal chatter, the never-ending noise within. A. Sujata in his book *"Beginning to See"* puts it this way: "If we think the noise of traffic is loud, we should go into a quiet room and listen to our minds". Whatever meditation is called, it brings peace and tranquility, increasing one's mental equilibrium.

Meditation helps us to let-go of fear. Most anxieties find their origin in some form of fear. Fear of being hurt, fear of losing a job, fear of losing money and possessions, fear of rejection, fear of failure, fear of losing a dear one, fear of old age, fear of death... Fear, fear, fear... Mostly fear about fear. We are afraid people.

When we are quietly brought face to face with our particular fear, we find that just by acknowledging it, it loses its power to frighten us. Meditation brings us in touch with love. Love for self, love for our near ones and so on in ever-widening circles. Love has no fear. Love gives us strength.

Meditation makes us realise that all experiences are lessons – no more, no less. We may experience sometimes bad, even shocking events, which are mentally de-stabilising but even such events may be transformed through meditation into positive milestones along the road to mental health and stability.

The Buddha says: "Everything is perfect, if only we care to see it". It seems too simple a statement and extremely difficult to accept when we are experiencing great distress. However, especially at such moments we must take our minds away from this anxiety – create a distance between the "I within" and the "I out there", who is so profoundly distressed. When we can do this , the Buddha's wisdom will gradually pervade our minds.

Meditation is letting-go of pre-conceived ideas. Answers will come to questions we did not even know we had. Searching for answers implies tension and the tension of that search will obscure knowledge as often we are looking for the answer we want, which is not necessarily the right one. All we need to do is, ask the question – be still and wait for the answer. It always comes when we are ready. Searching also signifies an outward-looking attitude. To find answers, we have to turn inward. If "I am That", then there is no need for a search. It is all within, not without.

The Indian poet, Rakindrath Tagore, expresses the same sentiments in the lines:

"Be still my heart and do not move your dust,
Let the world find its way to you."

Meditation makes us realise, that we cannot keep running away from ourselves. We waste an awful amount of energy doing just that. Meditation makes us face ourselves, seeing ourselves for what we are, it helps us to come to terms with ourselves, to understand ourselves.

It is in stillness, that we will become aware of who we are, where we are going, what it is we want to be and what it is we would like to achieve. Until such time that we know this, we will not discover our identity, define our destination, realise our ambitions, achieve our goal. We will be too scattered. **It is in stillness that this knowledge comes.**

Try to be still at least once a day. There seems to be a fear of stillness in this modern society. We surround ourselves with sound – the radio and T.V. which are often left on even when we are not listening or watching. Car radios, people walking and jogging wearing ear phones listening to their little pocket radio sets, are a sign of this "noise syndrome". When was the last time you called on someone and the house was still, although people were at home? Radios are now left on when no one is home in an effort to confuse would-be-housebreakers, as this is supposed to be an indication that someone is there! When were you last at home without the radio or T.V. going? Try it! Turn the radio or T.V. off, take the phone off the hook – the silence is deafening!

In *"Beginning to See"* A. Sujata says: "Meditation is for those who were born without having it all together". Since this would seem to include most of us, let us begin!

Unless there are reasons why you cannot sit cross-legged such as varicose veins, bad knees, arthritis, injury, try to sit in the traditional pose or kneel down and sit on the heels in Diamond posture. (part 3.) Main concern is that the spine is erect. This may present difficulties at first but we must work diligently at overcoming this, assisting ourselves at first by using cushions. If need be, sit leaning against a wall or use a straight-backed chair.

Checking the posture: the back is straight, the head aligned with the spine and as it were "balancing" on the neck, the chin is slightly inclined toward the chest, the hands resting, palms up, in the lap or comfortably placed on the knees. In that case, the tips of the thumb and forefinger are lightly touching in the Jnana Mudra.

The Jnana Mudra is a hand gesture. The thumb represents the spirit of the universe, the forefinger the spirit of self. When they form a circle, it signifies infinity or The Infinite. The three remaining fingers should be extended downward without tension. The eyes are closed and inward-looking toward the area of the Third Eye, just above the bridge of the nose in the centre of the forehead. Be sure not to create any tension.

Become aware of the body and relax every part of it without losing the posture. Begin with the feet and work upward to the head. The spine remains straight, the head in its original position. ACCEPT THE POSTURE. Repeat – again body awareness, holding the posture and letting go of tension in feet, legs, right up to the shoulders, the face (relax the jaws), the head.

If you are unable to sustain the steady posture and feel the need to move, do not worry about it. Without paying too much attention to the body, keeping the eyes closed, the head and shoulders as still as possible, move the part(s) which are complaining and assume the same or a more comfortable position. This does not have to interfere with your meditation. I observed this practice on my first trip to India, when our group visited an ashram in Puri which was devoted to teaching meditation. There were many European students resident there, so perhaps this practice was promoted to accommodate them. The knowledge that one can move if one needs to, often alleviates the necessity to do so as it is frequently our anxiety about holding the posture for a certain length of time, which makes it impossible.

Now begin to pay attention to the way you breathe. You are breathing quietly and comfortably..... Listen to your in - and exhalation..... Let the breath quieten, become slower, calmer..... Establish a rhythmical breathing pattern..... Feel the warmth and contentment of the moment you are in..... Observe the breath..... nothing else than breathing in and breathing out.....

After a while, pause for a moment at the end of the exhalation, even if it is only for a second. Inhale, exhale, pause... Inhale, exhale, pause... Then begin to concentrate on the pause, the quiet moment, when all seems still, only your heart-beat is discernable. Yoga says, that NOW is at the end of the exhalation before we decide to inhale again. Breathing in is saying YES to life, breathing out is flowing with the moment, the pause IS the moment – the NOW. Begin to hear: inhaling – "BE", exhaling "HERE", pause – "NOW"... inhaling – "BE", exhaling – "HERE", pause – "NOW"... BE... HERE... NOW... Continue until you feel you want to let-go of this and stillness will follow. No more breath awareness... no more inner sound... just being...

When you feel it is time to come out of the meditation, return your awareness to the breath and sit quietly for a while observing the breath flowing rhythmically. Gradually deepen your breathing and slowly become aware of the body. Keeping the eyes closed, very gently begin to move hands, shoulders, head, feet, legs and wherever you feel the need for movement. Then open the eyes, looking down first.

This is just an initial practice but will give you an idea of what it is like. There are two more meditations outlined elsewhere in this book. As with the relaxation in chapter 5, you may want to learn this meditation by heart, tape it or have someone read it to you.

Try to meditate in the same place and at the same time every day. Find a quiet place away from draught where you can be undisturbed. Having a special time each day avoids putting it off till later and then finding that another day has gone by without getting around to it.

Do not meditate after a meal, you'll find it difficult to lose body consciousness because of the activity in the digestive area. Also do not meditate just before going to bed. Meditation generates energy, keeps us alert, unlike relaxation which is great for inducing sleep.

A friend once complained to me, that she had trouble getting to sleep at night. "And I meditate every night before I go to bed" she said. "Sometimes I get up again and do some more meditating". She was surprised to learn, that she was effectively keeping herself awake!

There are many good books written on meditation. Else find yourself a teacher. This book is no substitute but perhaps an aide and I hope, a stimulant – a push in the right direction. Yoga is a very personal matter and it is therefore important to find a teacher with whom you are able to communicate, someone you feel comfortable with, someone you feel you can trust.

There are many forms of meditation. Meditation where the mind can wander freely, while you are the observer of its meanderings – meditation on a sound, called mantra meditation – meditation on an image such as a person you love or admire – meditation on an idea such as love, peace, harmony, contentment – meditation on an object of beauty or on scenery. Like a moonrise I once saw. We hear people describe a sunrise, well I saw a moonrise and it was magic!

The moon rose over a mountain ridge. The hills and the fields below it were all shades of green and brown, the sky, hues of blue and lavender. First there was a small area of light in an indentation in the ridge. This became a silver sliver and then the moon emerged as if by magic, till a large, perfectly round, silver ball seemed to rest on top of the mountain – only for a little while – as it continued its ascent. The "face in the moon" was so clear on this perfect summer's night that it seemed as if a kindly person looked out at me.

This would present a perfect scene for meditation, because although it was a "moving" scene in that the moon actually moved, there was such stillness in the movement, that the movement itself lost its impact. It seemed as if all creation was still, watching with me.

There is increasing evidence supporting the theory that meditation could have healing qualities. Some of this evidence is well documented. The late Dr. Ainslie Meares, who began advocating meditation as an alternative to more orthodox methods of curing disease, seemed for a long time like the proverbial voice crying in the desert. For years his colleagues turned a deaf ear, till finally, researchers into stress brought enough evidence forward to support

Dr. Meares' theories. Many people have been able to restore their health by learning his meditation technique. This seems to have consisted of evoking a profound stillness of which the meditator was only aware after, not during the meditation.

One of the most well-known cases in Australia is probably that of Ian Gawler. Ian Gawler writes in his book "You too can conquer cancer", how in January 1975 at the age of twenty five, he had his right leg amputated because of bone cancer. The cancer again manifested itself in November of that year and in March 1976 his specialist was of the opinion, that he had only two weeks to live. Ian went to Ainslie Meares and meditated five hours a day while he was in this critical stage of his illness, supported by his wife, Gayle. He also went on a special diet and tried other forms of alternative methods of healing. Ian Gawler is very much alive today. He is a practising veterinary surgeon, is very actively involved with support groups for cancer patients and gives lectures and workshops all over the country.

There are many stories like that. Even those people, who are not able to regain their health, invariably find that meditation gives them the strength and fortitude, which makes the consequences of their illness easier to bear and when death finally comes, their passing is a peaceful and joyous one.

I have been able to rid myself of quite a few physical problems. As I said in the beginning of this book, mine was a none too robust constitution. One problem however was quite major. After the birth of one of my children I haemorrhaged profusely, necessitating some surgical procedure, which resulted in cessation of ovulation and menstruation.

For years I practised daily visualisation, seeing Life Force flow into the uterus, making that organ whole again as well as concentrating on the pituitary gland. I had several check-ups by different doctors in the many countries we lived in. None could offer a solution except to say, as one prominent gynaecologist in New Zealand did, that is was highly unlikely that my periods would return after so many years (it was six years then).

Finally, after fourteen years, when I was forty one, my periods returned and were for several years as regular as when I was a young woman. My gynaecologist, a Macquarie Street specialist, called it a miracle and although not involved in Yoga himself, advised me to "keep up my practice". A year later when I went to see him for a check-up, he told me that he had discussed my case at an international gynaecological convention in Athens, as the return of menstruation after so many years is quite unheard of.

And then last year, we experienced the most convincing confirmation of the power of meditation and prayer. Our youngest daughter, Jane, mother of two children, Luke nearly five and Emily nearly two, was diagnosed to have a large growth in the upper left hand corner of the abdomen. Fifty two cat scan pictures and five X-rays, taken by different radiologists, eighteen days apart, as well as the two radiologists' reports, mentioning a "soft tissue mass", confirmed the doctor's diagnosis. An operation was deemed necessary after consultation with a surgeon.

Jane's G.P. told me before the operation, that the growth was massive, that she must have had this for at least a year, that whether it was malignant or not, it would have to be removed, as it would cause problems if it entered the bowel and that she was a very sick lady. (All his words)

Jane who had been unwell before, began to experience distinct discomfort and could no longer lie on her left side, which was visibly distended.

All the surgeon would say, when I spoke with him on the phone was, that "he had to go in" and that "he could not predict what he would do". He promised me however, to send word during the operation indicating what he had found and what action he proposed to take.

Gerald and I knew for the first time of the seriousness of Jane's condition on the night of Tuesday, August 26th (Jane had not wanted to worry us and interrupt our holiday!). The operation was scheduled for Monday morning, September 1st. We had less than a week.

On Wednesday morning I taught Jane, who up till then had shown no interest in Yoga or meditation, my simple healing meditation. She liked it and found it pleasant to do – she was on her way. Gerald and I had begun meditating the moment we heard; in fact, I don't think I slept more than two hours each night till the operation, as I felt that I could not afford to waste time sleeping, which I could spend meditating.

I contacted as many Yoga friends as I had time for under the circumstances and asked for their meditation. I phoned my family in New Zealand, who are devout Catholics. They began to pray, had Masses read and even enlisted the assistance of a whole convent of nuns! There were probably close to two hundred people involved in praying and meditating as a result of this "snowball effect"

When Jane was operated on on the Monday, the surgeon found nothing – no growth... NOTHING.

Her G.P., who before entering general practice had worked for five years with cancer patients, says, that he had been convinced that it was cancer and calls it "a mystery". "It will probably always remain a mystery", he said and he told me to "hang on to the X-rays, as they are the only proof we have, that something was there".

The joy we experienced was indescribable and when, the night after the operation, I sat by Jane's bed, her hand in my hand, I felt the luckiest, most priveleged and blessed person in the whole world!

Jane continues to be well. In fact, looking at her now, full of energy and her eyes shining, it is very obvious how unwell she was before the diagnosis. We often fail to "see" those closest to us properly till it is nearly too late. She has changed her diet, which left much to be desired since she left home and she practises meditation now. What a way to come to the Path!

The reactions to this happening: Quite a few people reacted with incredulity to the story of the growth disappearing. In fact, it seems as if they would prefer to accept, that all X-rays were wrong. Though why that should give them comfort is beyond me. Consider the implications if the diagnostic tool of the medical profession, which sends us into surgery would be so poor! At the other end of the scale were the Yoga meditators, who were not only happy for us, but also delighted and excited to see the power of meditation confirmed.

My family in New Zealand was not only happy, but accepted it with the faith with which they had approached God in prayer, saying , that "of course miracles still happen". After all, why ask for a miracle if you don't believe in the possibility of one occurring?"

Some people, although accepting the principle of meditation, had problems with the time factor. One friend, from whom I had least expected it, said, that he "did not understand the process".

Well, what is time? If we believe that God created the world in six days, resting on the seventh day, or as some say "in the blink of an eyelid", what, in comparison, is the disappearance of a growth in five days? If time is indeed all-embracing and not linear, if there is no past, and future, but only the present; if nothing has happened, but keeps on happening and we link into it as it happens, what is the problem? Why then are we so hung up on time?

Didn't the Buddha say: "Set your heart in one place and nothing is impossible"? He did not say "nearly everything is possible" or "quite a lot is possible", but "NOTHING is impossible". That means, that EVERYTHING IS POSSIBLE as long as "you set your heart in ONE place". And collectively we did just that! We did "set our hearts in **one** place"!

Relaxation and meditation supplies "time away from it all", without having to go through the trouble of having to book, pack and travel.

CHAPTER 8

THE LAUGHING YOGI

I would like to tell you about my meeting with the laughing Yogi, one of the most treasured memories of my first trip to India. I call him the laughing Yogi, as I don't even know his name.

Our group was staying in New Delhi and had received an invitation to participate in a Yoga session at the Yoga International Institute in Old Delhi, which started at 5.30 in the morning. We left the hotel at a quarter to five – only four of us had been enthusiastic enough to venture out at such an early hour. When we stepped into the taxi, we began to wonder about the wisdom of our decision, as it was extremely cold and very dark.

The taxi ride was an experience in itself! Our Sikh driver continued to switch the headlights off to, as he said, "preserve the car batteries". It was hair-raising to hurl through pitch dark Delhi in a cab without lights and a real test for our Yoga equilibrium! We still laugh about this adventure whenever we see each other – it certainly was a unique experience.

When we finally arrived – a little late, because of difficulties finding the place, we wondered whether we were at the right address. The sounds emanating from the place were like those of a market in full swing. This however, was the Yoga class in progress!

It was certainly the most unusual Yoga class I have ever attended. Imagine out in the garden on a small wooden platform, a group of men of all ages, some down from the platform in the grass. (The only woman present, was the teachers wife).

The teacher was virtually dancing with excitement and enthusiasm as he gave his instructions to the group in a loud voice. His students were laughing, making comments, coughing, spitting and groaning loudly when they found something difficult. Rather different from the atmosphere of peace and tranquility we try to create in the West!

If anyone had told me that I would feel at home in such a situation, I would not have believed it. But that is exactly what happened. There was so much joy there, so much naturalness, that I felt like a hand in a fitting glove – it felt right.

Toward the end of the session, the man whom I now call the laughing Yogi came forward. Picture him: a big man in his mid-thirties, a smile on his bearded face, sitting in the Lotus posture with the greatest of ease, who besides wearing a loose-fitting woollen jumper which had a large hole at one elbow, was sporting a knitted hat. Such an incongruous sight!

He invited us to sit cross-legged too and said:
"The emphasis in today's world seems to be on unhappiness, while we ignore and forget that there are so many things in life emanating happiness – the daily sunrise, birds in blossoming trees, beautiful butterflies on sweet-smelling flowers, the laughter of children... We should look at nature and smile and laugh more ourselves".

He then proceeded to introduce the following laughing exercise:
Sit in a cross-legged position, place your hands on your knees, breathe in through the nose, smile, and still smiling, exhale bend forward from the waist, taking the head toward the floor. Inhale, return to sitting position. No sound – do this three times.

Next breathe in through the nose, open the mouth slightly and breathing out again bend forward from the waist, taking the head toward the floor, laugh softly as if trying to suppress laughter – coming up again inhaling. Repeat this three times too.

After these preliminaries, laugh as loudly as you can while bending forward, and only return to your upright position when "coming up for air". From then on, you are free to do what you like. While belly-laughing, throw your arms in the air, slap your thighs, pound the floor, wipe your tears – let it all hang out!

The releasing power of this exercise is tremendous. I can still hear the sound of our laughter in the quiet, early morning. It was as if the whole of Delhi was reverberating with our unbridled joy.

After this merriment we sat completely still with our eyes closed and the class chanted a prayer... a poignant moment, touching us deeply.

This was the end of the Yoga session, after which everyone went to work. What a wonderful way to start the day! Compare this with the beginning of the day of some people you know or perhaps even with your own beginning of a new day.

Having needed perhaps a sleeping tablet to get to sleep, or feeling the after effects of too much eating and drinking the night before, which only a cup of strong black coffee seems to be able to remedy, many people are still in a state of fogginess the first few hours of the day.

We could all improve the quality of our lives by beginning the day in a more positive manner. If you feel good, it is easy to feel good toward others. As your tolerance increases, your relationships with other people will improve, making life so much more pleasant. As human relationships improve, the world will become a better place.

Now if you are used to taking sleeping tablets or tranquilisers, don't flush them down the toilet in a burst of enthusiasm and positivity. Give yourself time – **be patient.**

It is quite astounding how patient we can be with others, but how little patience we have with ourselves, And yet, I feel, that this is often the key to self-improvement. Don't be in a hurry, don't try to change overnight. Do it gradually – you have plenty of time – **you have the rest of your life!** Introduce Yoga into your daily routine and you will find that things will begin to "fall into place".

If you are feeling tense, check your breathing. The breath is a natural tranquiliser. It is impossible to be tense, anxious and agitated when the breath is flowing calmly, deeply and rhythmically. Don't think: "This may work for some people but nobody knows how I feel." "It is different for me – I was born that way." "No one knows what it is like to feel as I do." This may be true, but why not try deep breathing? What do you have to lose? The only side effects are positive ones!

Live each day as it comes. Take some time each morning to contemplate the day ahead. What would you like to achieve? What do you expect of it? At night, look back over the day. If it has been a good day, be pleased and tell yourself that tomorrow, is going to be another one like it. If the day was not so good, don't dwell on it, don't be discouraged, but see whether you can learn something from it. Then say to yourself: "Okay, this was today, which is already the past – tomorrow will be a better day". If you are living day by day like that, you will avoid biting off too large a slice of life at the one time, which can be very daunting. There are so many things we can imagine to go wrong. One day at a time is enough to cope with.

There is a lesson in the laughing Yogi's words. Indeed, there are still so many good things happening around us, so many good deeds by so many good people – so much positivity, although the news we are presented with daily appears to deny this. We seemingly never run out of bad news in the global village. T.V. and newspapers concentrate on bad news – alarming headlines sell more papers!

Let us not fall into the trap of accepting that what is presented as news, is reality. IT IS ONLY PART OF IT! Since good news is no news – since good news does not seem worth reporting, we are getting a distorted view of reality. This can become self-fulfilling as it induces a feeling of hopelessness and helplessness.

Of course, the laughing exercise is somewhat difficult to do by yourself. The family might think that you have cracked completely, already alarmed by your early morning attempts to get into the Lotus posture.

On the other hand, they may be intrigued by this very positive start of the day and like to join you in the laughter, suddenly realising that Yoga is fun.

The medical world is beginning to recognise the healing power of laughter. In the book *"Laugh after Laugh",* a Florida physician Dr. Raymond A. Moody, documents this with many instances of cases of remarkable recovery.

Then there is the book by Norman Cousins *"The Anatomy of an Illness".* In which he describes his recovery from a serious degenerative disease. He relates how he restored his health by laughing and by substituting vitamin C for his prescribed medication. His doctor was in favour of this experiment!

Laughter therapy is used in several hopitals in the U.S.: St. Joseph's Hospital in Houston, Texas; Decalb Cancer Hospital in Decatur, Georgia and Shawnee Medical Centre in Kansas City, Kansas. Laughter is promoted and encouraged by showing funny movies, visits by clowns, humorous books, etc. Special rooms are set aside for this purpose which are decorated in cheerful colours.

There are distinct physiological benefits from laughing: the muscles in the abdomen, chest and shoulders contract and the heart and pulse rate increase. Laughter has been termed "stationary jogging" by Dr. William Fry of Stanford University. The theory has been put forward that laughter relieves stress, stimulates the immune system and releases substances in the body which numb pain.

Earlier in the book I wrote that we not only have to digest what we eat, but also what we read and watch on T.V., inferring that negative or upsetting material can have a detrimental effect on our health. If we accept this, then it should not surprise us too greatly to learn that positive, uplifting books and T.V. programmes can have a beneficial effect on our health.

So it would seem that my laughing Yogi is a very wise man indeed! Laughter has been called "the doctor within". Michael Volin once said: "Laughter is the sunshine of the soul". **Let your soul bask in it!**

CHAPTER 9

IT IS NEVER TOO LATE...

The most wonderful aspect of yoga, in my view, is its total positivity – it is always holding out hope, no matter what one's mental or physical condition is.

Whatever your age, as long as you still have a functioning mind, you can come to grips with the situation you find yourself in – come to grips with sad, upsetting experiences, ill-health, afflictions resulting from ageing, etc.

It is never too late to take your destiny in your own hands, to take stock of your mental and physical health and take positive steps to bring some order in "the system". Don't dwell on the WHY of your mental/physical state. All you need to do is let go. Let the body get on with what it wants to do naturally – **being healthy.**

Apart from the dietary advice discussed in the second part of this book, please realise, that there is a form of Yoga to suit EVERYBODY.

Don't say to yourself: "I could never do this" – "I don't have the will power to do that!" Say instead: "I can try..." From there-on you will find, that the gentle path of Yoga brings gradual, but very noticeable benefits.

Try to find yourself a Yoga teacher who communicates with you on a level you understand, a level you find acceptable. Don't be discouraged if the search is not immediately successful. Every teacher develops her/his own style and personal empathy between you and that style is a very important pre-requisite for your development.

Above all, **be gentle with yourself.** That this feeling of inadequacy and stress is not a new phenomenon, becomes clear, when we read in the Desiderata:

> *"Beyond a wholesome discipline be gentle with yourself.*
> *You are a child of the universe, no less than the trees or the stars;*
> *You have a right to be here.*
> *And whether or not it is clear to you,*
> *No doubt the universe is unfolding as it should".*

Be patient! Realise, that it has taken you a certain number of years to get to the condition you are in now. It may take you the same number of days, weeks, months, or even years again to arrive at the point where you would like to be. Meanwhile your condition won't deteriorate which could be expected to happen without any action on your part. Instead, you will be improving and having a positive time.

Keep before your mind's eye what it is you want to achieve – visualise it daily. Whether it is answering your correspondence without too much delay or a twenty-four-inch waist (60cm centimetres doesn't sound the same somehow!), being kind and tolerant or becoming a chess champion. No matter what it is, be positively convinced and at the same time relaxed, that one day you will achieve your goal.

It took me ten years of daily practice to be able to sit in the Lotus pose, sixteen years to achieve the headstand, seventeen years before I was a vegetarian. But the joy, the personal joy is indescribable! Those who are perfect from the start, will never experience that joy. See, that "everything is perfect" as the Buddha said?

So don't be discouraged if it takes a while before you feel that you are getting somewhere. Don't look at people who seem to be doing things with the greatest of ease. Yoga is not competitive – we don't compare ourselves with others – we know that WE ARE ALL UNIQUE.

Yoga is no panacea for all ills. We can't be on cloud nine all the time. The art is not to be upset about being upset – not to be unhappy about being unhappy. We must be realistic; sometimes we have every reason to be upset or unhappy. Life is cruel at times. We all encounter sadness and distress. If we can find the courage and strength to face our problems squarely we are half-way on the road, not necessarily to happiness, but certainly to inner peace and tranquility, to equanimity and stillness within.

INTRODUCTION TO PART 2

When we talk of Life Force, we should realise that we speak of a real force: the universal energy. The universe is a large energy field – we are part of the universe and hence part of the universal energy stream, which should flow unimpeded through us. When we become ill, it means that we are no longer sufficiently in touch with that energy – that we are cut off to a degree. All we then have to do is to link in to that force again. It is the restoration of the natural breath and meditation which are the keys to **well being.**

No matter what our condition or illness is, our first priority is to restore the natural breath (see chapter 4).

The combination of energising breath and visualisation also becomes a very powerful tool for the purpose of pain management. Sometimes, when pain is particularly acute, it will seem like a white, searing entity. Don't consider this to be an enemy which has to be driven out. Instead "see" it as bright white energy and set about replacing the white searing pain energy with the bright white Universal Life Force Energy.

Don't say things like: "The pain is driving me crazy!" Don't even think it! Thoughts and words are vibrations and have an enormous influence on our physical and mental state. You can't afford to be driven crazy – you need your wits about you to be able to transform this pain bundle into a Life Force bundle!

Accept the pain – **relax** into it – BREATHE INTO the pain. Do not let the extreme disomfort of the body force you into a "mindless" experience. Try to bring the mind into play. Remember that tension creates "road closed" signs which deny entry to healing forces.

When pain becomes more manageable, panic will subside – the feeling of being out of control which is most unnerving, will disappear and we will be in charge of our destiny once more!

The next part of the book should not be read as a medical text book. Yoga does not offer cures for any ailment. There is no Yoga for ... **Yoga is not allopathic.** Yoga considers the whole person.

What you will read about in the next pages are remedies and practices which I have known to work, either through personal experience or through close observation. However, always ONLY with a Yogic approach and attitude.

This means that we first accept the condition we find ourselves in with total honesty and openness – WITHOUT FEAR. We will begin to understand that if we can lose our health, we should also be able to regain it. We are not attacked – we are in charge and we will KNOW THIS AS TRUTH.

This knowledge will come to us in stillness. I cannot emphasize enough the need to be still at least once a day.

Once we obtain this knowledge, we can begin to "set our hearts in one place" and, once again, get in touch with the Life Force, working diligently at our recovery, **the restoration of our health.**

SOME CONSIDERATIONS BEFORE STARTING YOUR YOGA PRACTICE

If you have any doubts about your physical condition, if you have spinal problems, are pregnant or have undergone surgery recently, **please consult your doctor** before commencing an exercise programme. However, you can always SAFELY practise the breathing, the relaxation and meditation as well as any movements from the segment "Exercises to be done while lying in bed". (part 3.) They will not interfere adversely with your state of health. In fact, you will find, that your rate of recovery will be accelerated.

Children can safely and with great benefit to themselves, practise all Yoga postures. However, Half Shoulderstand, full Shoulderstand and Triangular Rest pose are contra-indicated. The vertebrae in the neck are not fully developed yet and too delicate to cope with these postures.

Do not exercise shortly after a meal – let at least one and a half to two hours elapse. Exercising on a full stomach may induce indigestion and put too much strain on the heart. Early morning is the ideal time for your Yoga session.

There is no such thing as a **quick** Yoga practice. "Oh dear, it is already late – I have to do my Yoga yet!" Yoga should be practised slowly, with concentration on the breath and awareness of the body. It is more beneficial to do one posture properly than a few in a hurry. That is NO Yoga!

General rule for breathing is: When contracting the body, breathe out – when stretching/extending the body, breathe in. WHEN IN DOUBT, BREATHE OUT! You will never harm yourself while breathing out, while this is a possibility on the inhalation or when holding the breath in.

Guard against tension in all you are doing. There even can be tension in the way you approach your Yoga practice!

There is an in-built safety device in the muscles, which reacts to a sudden stretch with a reflex contraction like an instinctive "hold". By overstretching or "bouncing" to achieve a result, we are likely to activate this response. The muscle will be thwarted in its desire to elongate to its full potential. Therefore always stretch slowly, relax into the posture – accept the posture – let the exhalation take you there.

Relaxed muscles can be stretched a little further every time – a tense, taut muscle can very easily be injured.

Never force or strain; this will only lead to stiffness. You will have to work through this stiffness the next day.

Present a challenge to the body – no forcing, no pain, but an allowing; an accepting of the posture or movement. Let the exhalation take you there by relaxing into the posture.

At first it will be difficult to combine the awareness of the breath with the awareness of the body movement. However, it won't take long before this becomes second nature. This is one of the reasons why Yoga has such a calming influence on the mind. It is impossible to sustain awareness of the breath and the body movement and worry over other things as well!

Always begin your physical practice with a few stretches lying on your back on the floor. (part 3.) This aligns the spine and balances the posture.

Make sure to take a few deep breaths and to relax all muscles between postures and movements.

LISTEN TO THE BREATH – LISTEN TO THE WISDOM OF THE BODY.

EARLY MORNING ROUTINE

On waking up, go to the bathroom and empty the bladder. Then clean your tongue and throat. The tongue is an eliminating organ and during the night a certain amount of waste matter is deposited on the tongue and in the throat. Use an inverted spoon to scrape the tongue. Then gargle with lukewarm water and spit the water out. If you don't do this, you will swallow the waste matter which the body wants to get rid of, with your first sip! So much for the habit of a cup of tea while still in bed! After cleaning the tongue and throat, drink a large glass of water – warm in winter, lukewarm in summer. You may like to add a few drops of lemon juice to it.

Then lie on your back on the floor and do the stomach contractions as described in part 3 of this book. Udiyana and Nauli are highly recommended. You may like to ask your teacher to demonstrate those for you as they really have to be taught one to one.

When the breathing is comfortable again, sit in a cross-legged position with the back straight and do three rounds of Alternate Nostril Breathing. (part 3)

You are now ready for your early morning Yoga session. Make sure, to take a few deep breaths between postures. You don't need long rests nor relaxation, as you have been lying down and resting all night.

The morning practice differs from an evening session. In the morning we want to wake the body up, get it moving, whereas at night we want to wind down. If your main practice is in the morning, finish your day with a few stretches and a relaxation.

I would like to suggest, that you try to include:

Stretching lying flat on the back on the floor;

Breathing cycles to discourage coughs and colds;

Salute to the Sun;

Twist lying on the floor;

Spinal roll;

Cobra and/or Cat.

Finish with a standing or seated Cleansing Breath.

Then settle down for your meditation.

OTHER OPPORTUNITIES TO PRACTISE YOGA

People often make the remark that they would like to have a daily Yoga practice but that they just don't have the time. The concept of Yoga should be with us all day. Everything we do should be done in a Yogic way. Every time we move, we should do this with awareness and in combination with the breath. For instance hanging out the washing can be Yoga: Place the clothes basket on the ground and wind the clothes line up to such height that it can only be reached by stretching. Then proceed to inhale, stretching while pegging an article of clothing on the line – exhale, bending down to pick up a piece of clothing from the basket. Simple and effective, especially as the open air will make the breathing extra beneficial.

More examples: When travelling long distance in the car, stop at regular intervals and exercise the fingers and hands, bend the elbows, exercise the face and eyes, neck and shoulders. Walk around the car, do some knee-bends and bend forward and back. All this in combination with the breath. For most of these movements see under "Arthritis" part 2 and "Exercises to be done while lying in bed" part 3.

While waiting for a train or in a queue at the super market exercise feet and ankles, neck and shoulders.

When travelling long distance by plane, try to keep the feet elevated if possible. Take short walks along the aisles. When the lights are switched off, use the areas near the exits for a Yoga practice. Nobody will see you or take any notice. Sitting in your seat, keep the toes and ankles moving. This will avoid swollen ankles.

While watching T.V. sit on the floor – it is easier to keep your spine erect sitting cross-legged, than sitting in a so-called easy chair. This is a good opportunity to work on the legs and for giving yourself a foot massage.

At home place your telephone close to the floor, so that you can lie on the floor and put your feet up if someone should have an extended conversation with you.

These are only a few examples. I am sure that you will be able to think of many more!

SIMPLE HEALING MEDITATION

Sitting in meditation pose or lying down, (only if sitting up is physically impossible), establish energising breathing without undue effort. Breathe in and out several times to arrive at a comfortable rhythmical breath.

When the breath is calm, slow and deep and you feel ready, begin to visualise that Life Force flows into the affected body part on the inhalation, while on the exhalation, only the air leaves the body, taking the disease and all negativity with it.

Visualise the Life Force as a golden energy stream, or as a stream of bright white energy if you have problems seeing colours – the air on the exhalation is colourless. See the affected body part become a golden body part or a part of the body filled with bright white energy as more and more Life Force enters the body with each inhalation.

While visualising, say mentally "health" on the inhalation – "illness" on the exhalation; or on the inhalation "Life Force", on the exhalation "disease". Choose your own words – find what feels comfortable for you – even just "in" and "out". Verbalising helps to keep the mind focussed.

If visualising the Life Force presents difficulties for you, imagine it as warmth and feel the Life Force as a stream of warmth entering the affected part of the body.

This technique can equally successfully be applied to pain. Breathe Life Force into the pain and on the exhalation, consciously relax the area where the pain is. Tension increases pain sensation.

Meanwhile be mindful that there is no "pushing" or "willing" on the exhalation. Welcome the Life Force when you breathe in and "let go" of the disease or pain when you breathe out. TRUST, that by opening yourself to the Life Force and by not hanging on to the illness or pain, you are allowing the healing to take place – that you will indeed be healed. KNOW that this is so!

As you are breathing slowly and regularly, "see" the part of the body filling with Life Force. When the body part is filled with Life Force, see it begin to overflow as more and more Life Force is added with each breath – see it stay around that part of the body like a protective layer, like an aura.

Do this for at least twenty minutes each time and when a situation is serious, spend as much time as possible in meditation. Sometimes it is advisable to go away by yourself, letting solitude assist the meditative process.

When we meditate for someone else, we should visualise the person – see her or him clearly before us. Then we let the life Force stream into us on the inhalation and, on the exhalation, we send the Life Force through the heart centre to the person we are meditating for. We can either direct the Life Force to the whole person – see her/him bathe in it – or we can "target" the specific organ or part of the body to be healed.

Ideally, we sit in a quiet meditation pose, but we can do this just as effectively while we are working and going about our daily duties. You know of course, that the purpose of the practice of meditation is always to be meditating – always to be in touch with the still centre within.

A LONGER MEDITATION

As with all meditation, sit or lie in the posture described earlier. Refer to chapter 7. Relax the body as before and mentally prepare yourself to be still for at least twenty minutes. If you feel the need to move, please do not feel a failure; you will improve with practice!

Most things in life are experienced through our senses – through seeing, hearing, touching, smelling, tasting. In order to come to a deeper level of meditation in this session, we will practise pratyahara, which is withdrawal of the senses.

Sitting or lying quietly, become aware of your breathing. Slowly breathe in and slowly breathe out. No special effort, but a distinct in and exhalation, establishing a comfortable breathing rhythm.

Then begin to feel as if the breath travels up along the spinal cord on the inhalation and down again on the exhalation. Inhaling – from the lowest vertebra all the way up into the head where the delicate vertebrae are and exhaling – reverse, from the top vertebra all the way down to the coccyx. Repeat this for several breaths.

After a while, knowing that Life Force enters the body with each breath, see the Life Force surging up along the spine with each inhalation, down again on the exhalation. Visualise it, feel it, experience it. Continue this for several breaths.

Now add sound to this. Mentally hear or say "So" on the inhalation, "Ham" on the exhalation. So Ham – That I am, I am That. I am part of creation, part of the universe, part of the cosmos. I am part of everything and of everyone – I am part of all there is. So Ham – That I am.

After a while, let go of the breath..... let go of the images..... let go of the sound..... Let the breath come as it comes, no more effort..... no more concentration on, no more awareness of and no more involvement with the breath.....

Then withdraw your sight – you are looking inward; withdraw your sense of hearing – you are listening to your inner sound, your inner music, your inner voice; withdraw your sense of touch – you are getting in touch with yourself; withdraw your sense of taste and of smell. You are going inward into the great stillness, which is within all of us.

Sometimes you may find that it is as if you hear soft music playing. Perhaps it is as if you are in a small chapel, a small light in the distance, where it feels as if the peace embraces you. Other times it may feel as if you have entered a large cathedral. You found the door open on a week day and sitting there quietly, you become aware of the vibrations of all the people who have been there before you. Who have come there with their joys and sorrows. They are the people, who have touched your life or whose life you have touched and who have become part of you.

Perhaps you will have many other experiences. Let them come – do not have any emotions about them – just observe.

Then let the stillness take over... KNOW THAT YOU ARE...

Coming out of the meditation, return your attention to the breath. As the mind returns to the body, slowly begin moving the body again; shoulders, wrists, hands. Then open the eyes looking down first and move the rest of the body.

AIR

The question is often asked whether deep breathing is a healthy activity if one lives in a city with all the disadvantages of air pollution. Of course, breathing in fresh country air is preferable over inhaling polluted air and it is obvious that if we are in a car behind a truck or bus which emanates large black clouds of smoke, it makes good sense to close the window and to go right down to a very shallow breathing pattern till the situation is no longer acute.

If you live in the centre of a city where air pollution is high, keep windows facing roads closed if at all possible and open the windows at the rear of the house. Try to practise in a room to the rear.

Also realise that during deep energising breathing we not only breathe in deeply but we also breathe out fully; something which not many people do habitually. By emptying the lungs as much as possible, there is little build-up of grime and grit in the lungs and there are no "dead areas". It would seem that there is more pollution left in the lungs of a shallow breather than in the lungs of someone practising energising breathing.

Furthermore, it is not only the depth of the breath which benefits us but also the tempo, the rhythm. Shallow breaths are of necessity quicker, resulting in an agitated mind.

ARTHRITIS

The consequences of arthritis can be very debilitating. However, from observation it would seem, that we are not altogether helpless – we need not despair.

Gerald's maternal grandmother had severe arthritis, his mother too was plagued by the disease and his younger sister has trouble with her hands. So when he began to show signs too, he was quite worried. Ten years ago his hands were so bad, that he had difficulties in the morning putting his fingers around the steering wheel of his car.

When the acute stage was over, he started gentle Yoga exercises as well as breathing and visualisation. He also started to take this magic potion:

Dissolve a teaspoon of honey in half a glass of boiling water – fill the glass with cold water to make it luke-warm. Add one teaspoon of double strength apple cider vinegar. Drink this before breakfast.

It is an old remedy and it was handed on to Gerald by an old man in New Zealand. It has certainly helped him and many others to whom we recommended it. An advantage is that it is totally natural and unlike some prescribed medication, has no negative side effects, but benefits other aspects of the body's metabolism as well.

I would like to tell you about Irene, who has been a Yoga student of mine for thirteen years. Twelve years ago she planned to have her feet operated on, because they were extremely painful due to arthritis. Just then Irene's husband was diagnosed to have leukaemia and she felt, that she could not afford the time to sit around recuperating with two bandaged feet, so she cancelled the operation.

Instead Irene made some changes to her diet – she cut out all salt, sugar and red meat, eating very little cheese. During her daily Yoga practice, she began to concentrate on those movements she felt would benefit her feet, knees and hands, which were also problem areas. The consequences of arthritis (pain and stiffness) have disappeared to such a degree, that she has been able to manage without the medication she was on for seven years.

I often call Irene indomitable or irrepressible. Before I wrote this down, I looked those words up in the dictionary. Indomitable means "stubbornly persistent" and irrepressible "not to be repressed or restrained". That gives you the real picture!

Irene's husband passed away eight years ago and a year later she broke her right knee in two places – Irene was in her sixties then. The surgeon predicted, that she would most probably always need a walking stick. Irene exercised the knee daily and that knee is less troublesome now than her left knee!

I am telling you this story, because it underscores my theory, that we are not hopeless, helpless people. We are in control! However, we do have to decide that we want to get better and work diligently at it.

Do not exercise when the condition is acute. REST, RELAX, VISUALISE. When the pain is bad, rub some Deep Heat or similar ointment into the afffected area at night – wrap some flanellette cloth around it. This will alleviate some of the pain and will also allow the muscles around the joint to relax. A natural reaction is to become tense in the afflicted area, which will only aggravate the condition.

As soon as pain permits, gently exercise the joints, so that the muscles around the joints do not become weak. Gentle movement stimulates the production and circulation of synovial fluid around the joints.

Exercising in water is highly recommended as buoyancy decreases the weight of the body on the joints. Because seawater is denser, it is preferred over fresh water.

Try the "Exercises to be done while lying in bed" (part 3). If possible do them lying on the floor. Use a Yoga mat or folded blanket for "cushioning"

Sleep on a firm bed; sagging mattresses aggravate the condition.

Include celery in your diet – drink fresh celery and carrot juice. Celery seeds make a very pleasant "tea".

Avoid coffee and tea and most specifically red wine, which according to Gerald's G.P. is "poison" for people with arthritis.!

People with rheumatoid arthritis have also greatly benefitted from this regimen.

Suggested movements encouraging flexibility in the knees:

Knee bends 1: Stand with feet parallel and at shoulder width, arms by the sides. Inhale – while raising the arms overhead come onto the toes; exhale – lower the arms while bending the knees till you sit on the heels (stay on the toes); inhale – raise the arms while straightening the knees and stand on the toes again; exhale – while lowering the arms, come back to the heels. Make this a continuous movement.

Do not move the knees further apart – keep them in line with the feet. If you have difficulties maintaining your balance, hold on to a wall or the back of a chair with one hand while raising the opposite arm. Change sides.

Knee bend 2: Stand with feet parallel and at shoulder width, arms by the sides. Keep heels on the floor throughout. Inhale – bend and straighten the knees, swing both arms up; exhale – bend and straighten the knees, swing both arms down. Make this a continuous movement.

Make the knee bends as deep as possible without taking the heels off the floor and make the arm movements loose-swinging. This is quite different from the raising and lowering of the first exercise. Be sure to move with the breath.

Rotation: Sit on the floor, bend the right knee, place both hands behind the thigh just above the knee and hold the thigh close to the chest. Try to hold this postion as you rotate the lower part of the leg. Inhale – straighten the leg upwards, pointing the toes; exhale – describing a large circle begin to move the foot to the right and then down; inhale – rotate the foot to the left and up till the leg is straight again; exhale. Repeat this two times also rotating anti-clockwise. Other leg.

Movements to combat stiffness in the shoulders and neck:

Draw the shoulders up toward the ears – hold. Bring the left ear toward the left shoulder – make the head heavy and let it rest on the shoulder. Make sure to hold the shoulders as high as you can.

Gently return the head to the centre. Bring the right ear toward the right shoulder – make the head heavy and let it rest on the shoulder. Again, make sure to hold the shoulders as high as possible.

Slowly return the head to the centre. Keeping the shoulders high and neck elongated, pull the chin toward the notch in the throat and gently bring the head forward. Hold.

Again return the head to the centre. Continue to hold the shoulders high and slowly bring the head back, letting it rest on the shoulders. Feel how the back of the neck is squeezed and the throat is stretched. Hold.

Return the head to the centre and lower the shoulders. Shrug the shoulders till all stiffness is gone.

This is a head rotation which is completely safe and most effective. Because of the delicate nature of the vertebrae in the neck, take care to do all head movements SLOWLY and continue rhythmical breathing.

ASTHMA

Yoga means good news for people with asthmatic tendencies. In fact, it is the best news they are ever likely to receive! The consequences of an attack can be totally negated or else greatly alleviated. I have observed this from very close quarters.

Our second daughter Alice, developed asthma at the age of ten after frequent bouts of bronchitis. Her case was quite severe. We had no experience with this illness and felt totally out of our depth. It was very frightening to see her labour for air and panic reigned all round. That this made her condition worse is beyond doubt!

Our G.P., who had an asthmatic child himself, was a source of great strength to us. I began to read up on the disease, especially in Yoga books and began to experiment with certain Yoga breathing cycles. From a physiotherapist I learned a lung massage and I also excluded certain food items from Alice's diet.

Now at twenty seven, Alice has not had an attack since she was fourteen. Of course, the tendency remains; when Alice gets a cold it often seems to settle in her chest. But then, she does not have many colds due, no doubt, to her breathing practices.

Another case I was closely involved with was a student of mine in her mid-fifties. Jacky had been and asthmatic since childhood and had spent a year in hospital when she was twenty eight. After being discharged, she had needed help in the home as she was unable to do much physical work. She had been on cortisone ever since. Jacky practised the Yoga breathing exercises faithfully every day and her specialist was astounded at her progress, allowing her to reduce her medication gradually. It was exciting to observe her improved health.

To avoid having to use the cumbersome method of referring to the asthma patient as he/she and using the words his/her, I shall from hereon speak of he and him, but am of course not only addressing myself to male asthma patients.

A great deal depends on how serious a patient (or the patient's parent) is about wanting a cure and how dedicated he becomes to his practice. To be effective and to obtain the desired results, the exercises need to be practised daily.

It is important to understand what the specific problems of an asthmatic person are. Such a person habitually breathes high in the chest and takes short, frequent breaths. The lower parts of the lungs are hardly used. This breathing habit is reflected in the body; the shoulders slightly forward hunched, the lower chest caved in. This posture in itself prohibits natural breathing.

When, through an allergic reaction or cold, phlegm is produced in the bronchi, spasms result which inhibit the flow of air even more. The patient feels as if he cannot breathe in when, in fact, he has problems breathing out! Panic and fear make him "blow himself up" as it were, with short frequent inhalations, hardly exhaling at all. A typical phenomenon at this stage is the distended nostrils which show the desperate effort the patient is making to obtain air.

Panic and fear are worsening the attack and those around the patient should do all they can to put his mind at rest. Once the patient knows how to breathe properly, he begins to feel in control of the situation and the fear will subside to a large degree. This will assist to alleviate the severity of an attack.

Asthmatic people often seem to be "mouth breathers". This should be discouraged as the air thus inhaled has not been warmed, filtered and humidified as it would be if it were inhaled through the nose. Mouth breathing itself can trigger off an attack. Apart from the daily Yoga practice, swimming is highly recommended as long as care is taken not to become chilled.

If you have an asthmatic child, become a team with him. Don't let him tackle the problem on his own. Do the exercises with him every day. So that when he has an attack, he has you to be with him, telling him to breathe out... breathe out... breathe out... If the attack comes during the night, divert his attention – play a game or read him a story. When all is dark, things seem worse and fear arises easily, aggravating his condition.

Consider his diet. Avoid all phlegm-producing foods such as cream, whole milk, ice cream, cheese and chocolate. Good substitutes are: skim milk, buttermilk, non-fat yoghurt, cottage cheese, goat's milk. If you want to give him a special treat, give him a Carob bar available from the health food store. Avoid monosodium glutamate as this often induces an attack.

The following regimen restored Alice to perfect health. I believe this happened because Yoga goes to the core of the illness whereas medication usually treats only the symptoms of an illness.

If you would like to follow the suggested routine but are in doubt as to your over-all state of health – if you are an older person, have a heart condition or hypertension, **please consult your doctor first.**

The patient should be tipped upside-down first thing in the morning. To do this, make sure that he does not sit up on awakening, but from a lying-down position let him roll onto the stomach, hanging head-down from the waist over the side of the bed. Supply him with plenty of tissues and leave him to hang for a few minutes. People with **high blood pressure** should **monitor carefully** how they feel about the **inverted position.**

You are going to pat his back while he is hanging forward over the bed. To do this "cup" your hands, closing the fingers and slightly rounding the hands. The air will be caught between your hands and the patient's back, making a hollow sound.

Pat his back from the lower lungs to the top of the lungs; in other words:from just above the waist to just below the shoulders. Do this several times encouraging him to cough whether he wants to or not. THIS IS IMPORTANT. You will be surprised at the result! If there is any phlegm anywhere, it will be brought up, as it has not had the chance yet to go right down into the lower lobes of the lungs. This will avoid a great deal of coughing later during the day.

Let him rest for a little while in this position. Then place your hands around his lower ribcage and as he breathes out, push the ribcage inward while vibrating the hands. The exhalation is through the mouth with a haaaaa sound. Do this several times too, then let him rest lying on his back till the breath is back to normal.

The deep breathing Yoga class in session.

Practise the following breathing cycles:

Sit in a comfortable cross-legged position or Diamond Pose (see part 3.) with the spine erect. Remember that it is impossible to breathe properly when slouching. It is beneficial to have the sun shine on the chest, even if it is through a window. Make sure to take several slow deep breaths between each section. Do not start a new set before the breath has returned to its normal rhythm. **Visualise the Life Force to stream into the chest with each inhalation.**

Your FIRST CONSIDERATION IS THE RESTORATION OF THE NATURAL BREATH as discussed in chapter 4. This alone will greatly improve the condition.

1.– Practise three rounds of Alternate Nostril breathing (part 3).

2.– Apply chin lock: Keeping the back of the neck elongated, pull the chin into the notch in the throat. Keep the spine erect and breathe in and out through the nose; slowly and deeply. Ten breaths.

The following manipulations with the hands are done by the patient himself, although a parent can do them for a young child:

3.– Breathe in deeply – hold the breath and tap the top of the chest with the finger tips – breathe out through the mouth – haaa. Do this three times.

3a. Breathe in deeply – hold the breath and rub the lower lung area vigorously with the palms of the hands – breathe out through the mouth – haaa. Repeat three times.

3b. Breathe in deeply – hold the breath and pat the lower lung area with "cupped" hands – breathe out through the mouth – haaa. Repeat three times.

3c. Breathe in deeply – hold the breath, bend slightly forward and let the loosely closed fists fall to the area of the lungs in the back – breathe out through the mouth – haaa. Repeat three times. Take care NOT to hit the area below the ribcage!

4.– Blowing up imaginary balloons: Breathe in deeply – breathe out through **pursed lips.** It is important that the patient tries to expel ALL air from the lungs. Let him therefore visualise the balloon and try to "blow it up" as large as possible. Do not force – this is quite strenuous. Make sure to normalise the breathing by taking a few slow deep breaths before "blowing up the next balloon".

5.– "Being a steam engine": Breathing rapidly in and out through a slightly open mouth. Use your own discretion as to how long this can be continued. It is counter-productive to become too tired.

Standing up:

1.– Practise three rounds of the cleansing breath. (part 3)

2.– Bend the arms, place the hands on the shoulders, elbows out sideways. Breathe in – hold the breath – pull the shoulders toward the ears – apply chin lock – bring the elbows toward each other and **squeeze** – holding the posture as long as possible. Release on exhalation. Visualise to squeeze air out of the lungs like water out of a sponge – "see" phlegm leave the lungs on the exhalation. Take as many slow deep breaths as are necessary to return the breathing to normal. Repeat three times.

These breathing cycles take around ten to fifteen minutes to do – not much if we consider what is at stake! I cannot emphasize strongly enough the importance of doing this

DAILY. Alice once said to me: "I would have grown up to be a fat asthmatic if you had not been my mother." I hope that your child will say that to you one day – it will be worth all your trouble!

Children who are too young to do these breathing exercises, should be up-tipped first thing in the morning. The parent can do this by placing a cushion on the lap and letting the child hang forward from there. It gives the child a greater sense of security to be close to the parent.

They can blow up real balloons. As this is a difficult enough task for an adult, present him with some "old" balloons, which have been blown up several times before, otherwise they may lose interest.

A favourite game of little ones, is blowing cottonwool balls across the table.

Suggested Postures:

Cobra – Half Shoulderstand – Fish posture – Camel posture (part 3)

BAD POSTURE

Avoid sitting in "easy chairs". These are not as comfortable as they are supposed to be and certainly very rarely encourage correct posture. Make it a habit to sit on the floor in a cross-legged position or with the legs straight out forward. If this presents difficulties, support yourself against a wall.

Suggested: Stretches on the floor, keeping the arms as close to the floor overhead as possible and Spinal Roll. See part 3.

BAD SKIN

Best remedy for bad skin is fresh air and water – lots of it! To obtain the first, see that the natural breath is restored (see chapter 4.). Try to do your breathing sessions outside, early in the morning when the air is still clean. Avoid smoke-filled rooms and, of course, do not smoke yourself.

When you do your breathing sessions, visualise the Life Force to go to the afffected areas.

Drink plenty of water and avoid constipation. Bathing in seawater has been known to be successful.

Avoid in your diet the following foods: white flour and white sugar, fats, cream, whole milk and cheese, deep-fried foods, chocolate, cocoa, coffee and alcohol. Use fresh vegetables – raw is preferred, citrus fruits, skim milk, non-fat yoghurt and cottage cheeses.

Take a teaspoon full of brewer's yeast or tarula yeast each day. This is an acquired taste (!), but it does help.

Have a Yoga relaxation at least once a day as some people get pimples when they are nervous. On the other hand, you would become nervous when you are constantly breaking out in pimples!

Read also "Diet", "Constipation" and "Water". (part 2)

BOWEL UPSET – DIARRHOEA – VOMITING

Here follows a very old remedy which my mother used whenever we had problems in this area. When I was around eight years old there was a dysentery epidemic in Amsterdam. I remember it so well, because two of our young friends in the street where we lived, died as a consequence of this illness. We were on mum's remedy for days!

I have used it for my children when they were sick and so have most of my friends for theirs. I have never known it not to work. In fact, I took a large bottle to the hospital for Jane recently when she could not stop vomiting after the operation. She had about three quarters of it and the lady in the bed next to her finished it off. Both felt much better for it.

Boil up a quantity of rice in a great deal of water. Let it boil till you are left with very sticky rice and thick, glutonous ricewater. Drink this fluid as often as you can. It has all the food value of the rice but not the roughage. You can exist on it for quite a while if need be. An advantage is, that it can be offered to tiny ones in a bottle.

Drink plenty of fresh water – relax and rest.

See a doctor if the condition does not improve. BE ESPECIALLY CAREFUL WITH LITTLE ONES – LOSS OF FLUID IS VERY DANGEROUS.

CHEST COLDS and COUGHS

See the special breathing cycle under Asthma (part 2). See also part 3 under "Breathing practice to discourage chest colds and coughs".

CONSTIPATION

This is quite a common complaint especially among the not-so-young. This can be extremely uncomfotable and sometimes even painful. Constipation is much more prevalent than is often realised. People who have one bowel movement each day could still fall into this category as, ideally, we ought to pass everything we eat within twenty four hours. Having a more sluggish metabolism can be detrimental to our health.

Through insufficient vacating of the bowels, the waste matter lingers far too long in the body, some of the toxic material escapes through the porous walls of the bowel and is re-absorbed by the body.

Resorting to laxatives makes the bowels lazy and interferes with the absorption of nutritious matter by the body. Constipation often causes haemorrhoids or makes existing ones worse.

I should know all the tricks of the trade because (you guessed it!) I had problems in that area too. In fact, I was a constipated child. On occasions when it seemed completely hopeless, my mother would give me a soap suppository. I remember this vividly because of the distress this caused me. I used to cry loud and long!

This condition stayed with me while growing up, although I was able to keep it under control as long as I did nothing out of the ordinary. However, I only needed to go on a holiday, be sick or have a stay in hospital and I was in trouble on the second day. During my first pregnancy, constipation just about spoiled the whole event for me.

The sister nursing me after my first baby was born, gave me a few hints which I gladly pass on to you:

1.– When you feel the urge to go, when the peristaltic movement inside becomes evident, DON'T POSTPONE – GO!

2.– Once on the toilet, take your time – bring a book or magazine.

3.– When you have trouble passing a motion, breathe in and push gently on the held breath as if compressing a cushion of air. Relax on the exhalation and repeat.

I never had problems any more after taking up Yoga. Suggested exercises and asanas: Head to knee and Stomach contractions (part 3) and Pelvic tilting (Pregnancy part 2)

Make sure there is sufficient fibre in your diet (see under "Diet" part 2). Sometimes eating a few prunes each day or drinking prune juice is helpful. **Drink plenty of water.**

If your constipation is caused by a congenital defect, please seek the advice of your doctor.

CRAMPS AND TINGLING IN LEGS AND FEET

Especially young children and teenagers suffer from cramps, often occurring during the night after a day of physical exertion. Sports carnivals and competitions are notorious for causing this phenomenon.

The cramp may be due to loss of salt through heavy perspiration in hot weather. Suggested is to drink a glass of some (very slightly) salted water during exercising. Drink plenty of fresh water and avoid cola drinks.

To alleviate a cramp: stretch the affected muscle and massage the leg. Rub Deep Heat or a similar cream into the affected leg.

To avoid getting cramps: keep feet and legs warm – do some gentle foot, ankle and knee exercises before going to bed, (see "Exercises to be done while lying in bed" part 3) and check vitamin B and calcium levels in the body.

Tingling in legs and feet in adults is sometimes called "restless leg syndrome". This does not seem much of a complaint, but according to people plagued by it, it is something one gets up for in the middle of the night – apparently it is quite impossible to ignore as there may be a burning or prickling sensation.

Often this condition seems due to poor circulation in the legs. Many have found great relief through knee bends and other knee bending exercises (see under "Arthritis" part 2)

Also "cycling" or vigorously shaking the legs while in the Half Shoulderstand has been known to work (Half Shoulderstand part 3). For a full explanation of the "cycling", read paragraph 6 under "Haemorrhoids, etc, (part 2). If the

Half Shoulderstand presents difficulties, elevate the legs while lying flat on the back and shake the legs and "cycle" in that position.

Taking the apple cider vinegar and honey potion has also brought relief (see "Arthritis" part 2).

Another cause for these complaints can be hardened and clogged arteries. If you suspect this, please consult your doctor and ask for a thorough check up. Also see under "Heart Complaints" (part 2)

Drink plenty of fresh water. Avoid blood vessel constricting substances such as coffee, tea, cola drinks and tobacco. Alcohol too should be avoided as it slows the blood circulation and converts to saturated fat.

Practise relaxation, visualisation and meditation.

CYSTITIS – INCONTINENCE – KIDNEY PROBLEMS – SWOLLEN ANKLES

I am particularly familiar with cystitis as at one stage of my life I was chronic with it. It seemed as if I had just had an attack, was having one or was on the way to getting one – it was debilitating!

Then I turned a corner. It was when I had my second cystoscopy that the specialist advised me to change my drinking habits. (water !!) I should say non-drinking habits, because that is what it amounted to. I hardly drank any fluids at all. My father used to say that I was like a chook – apparently they don't drink much either.

The urologist advised me to drink a large glass of water every time I went to the toilet. The first few days I felt most uncomfortable – I could virtually hear the water slosh around inside me as I moved – I felt water-logged!

However, this meant the end of my affliction. Of course, Yoga too advocates drinking at least nine glasses of water each day. It was just that the message had never penetrated!

Cystitis is inflammation of the urethra and the bladder. Symptoms are a frequent urge to urinate and a painful, burning sensation when passing water. Sometimes the urine is cloudy or has traces of blood in it.

Avoid highly spiced foods, coffee and tea. Smoking too should be avoided as this tends to make the urine more concentrated.

More women that men seem to suffer from this complaint. If men experience the symptoms mentioned earlier, this may be due to an enlarged prostate gland. As this increases in size, it presses on the neck of the bladder causing problems with the emptying of the bladder. This can lead to weakening of this organ and infection in the kidneys. Medical investigation is warranted in both cases in order to establish the cause of the discomfort.

As the specialist explained, through lack of fluids the urine becomes so concentrated that the kidneys have difficulty coping with it. Also the bladder is adversely affected by this concentrated urine, finding it difficult to pass. Each infection in the bladder can cause a scar tissue build-up in the urethra, narrowing this passage, thereby making subsequent infections more likely.

Use little or no salt in your cooking – certainly ban the salt shaker from your dining table. There are substitutes available at healthfood stores.

Incontinence is also often helped by drinking plenty fluids. Flushing the system through makes it more vigorous. Strengthen the pelvic floor to avoid losing the tone in the sphincter muscles. See under "Pregnancy" part 2. and "Stomach Contractions" part 3. When resting or sitting quietly, tighten and release the muscles in the pelvic floor several times. "Interrupting the flow" while urinating is an excellent exercise too.

Suggested asanas: Cobra – Half Locust as backward bending massages the kidney area. (part 3)

Swollen ankles can be due to fluid retention. Check with your doctor to establish the cause.

Suggestions:

Lose weight if necessary,
Use salt sparingly,
Drink plenty of fresh water, (9 glasses p. day recommended)
Put your feet up as often as possible – avoid standing in one spot for any length of time.
Practise inverted postures as indicated for varicose veins.

Although diuretics may have to be prescribed initially in order to cope with the problems inherent in fluid retention, if possible, endeavour to minimise the number of tablets taken, as using large amounts of diuretics should be avoided.

Of course check your breathing to see that you are breathing correctly and use visualisation to obtain your goal.

DIABETES

People who have diabetes will find great benefit from a regular Yoga practice, as it is important for them to be physically active in order to use up the excess sugar in the bloodstream.

As diabetic patients need to be very disciplined about what kind of food they eat, as well as when they eat it, the discipline of the daily Yoga practice will permeate their lives and will make the regular injections or tablet taking seem less tedious. Also, eating when you NEED to rather than when you WANT to; not what you WANT to but what you NEED to, will seem less of a "straight jacket".

Daily stomach contractions described in part 3 are excellent as are Nauli and Udyana which are better taught by a teacher one to one.

Practise the two following postures daily:

1.– Sit in Diamond posture (part 3). Make fists of the hands, thumbs inside. Bend the elbows and place the elbows on the abdomen on either side of the navel. Place the forearms along the thighs, the fists close to the knees.
Inhale – exhale – bend forward bring the head toward the fists press the elbows into the abdomen; inhale – return to sitting position; exhale. Repeat three times building up to six times.

2.– Sit in Diamond posture. Make fists of the hands, thumbs inside and place the fists on either side of the navel. Inhale – exhale – bend forward toward the knees while pressing the fists into the abdomen; inhale – return to sitting position; exhale. Repeat three times building up to six times.

It would seem that the mental and emotional state of the person with diabetes, has a great influence on his physical condition.

Our eldest grandson Anthony (13) has had diabetes since he was five years old. We have found time and again, that when he is happy and mentally on an even keel his readings are much more stable than when he is upset or depressed.

Practise balancing postures (part 3) as these increase the equilibrium. Relaxation, visualisation and meditation are highly recommended.

DIET (well-balanced, healthy).

A sensible diet is a prerequisite for a happy family life.

For a diet to be well-balanced and healthy, it should include all food components: protein, carbohydrates, fat, minerals and vitamins. Besides this, it is very important, that there is bulk supplied by eating plenty "roughage". Have some unprocessed bran on your regular breakfast cereal. Soak it in fruit juice or milk or mix it with yoghurt. If your first reaction is that it resembles pig slop, don't worry, you will soon acquire a taste for it!

More roughage: eat fruit in the skin where possible, raw carrots (if your teeth are beyond carrot-eating, slice or grate them), raw celery and cauliflower, capsicums, cucumbers.

Substitute wholemeal flour for white flour, brown rice for white rice (more fibre), honey or raw sugar for the white refined variety.

Have a few meatless meals each week. Eat fish, lentils, soya beans, nuts or eggs. Buy some soya protein or tofu at the healthfood shop.

Steam your vegetables and keep the water for soups or drink it. Boil potatoes in the skin.

Eat less fat. The over-use of animal fats is one of the reasons for the high incidence of heart disease in the West.

Avoid foods with colouring and/or preservatives – read the labels!

I find it a good idea not to mix fruit and vegetables at the same meal for reasons of digestion. I have fruit with my lunch and vegetables with my dinner. This does not mean, that I become anxious when I am offered a fresh fruit salad for dessert at a dinner party!

Drink plenty of fresh water – at least nine glasses per day. However, avoid drinking while having a meal. This interferes with the digestion of your food. Drink no later than half an hour before meals and let at least an hour go by before you drink again after meals.

DROWSINESS

I have heard the theory put forward that drowsiness in elderly people and disabled patients in wheelchairs can be attributed to insufficient consumption of water. This is believed to cause hardening of parts of the brain matter. Suggested is to drink at least nine glasses of water per day. If you need assistance when going to the toilet, it is understandable that you begin to cut the intake of fluids down. However, this creates other problems. Consider going to the toilet to be an exercise and not an insurmountable hurdle.

Another cause of drowsiness can be bad posture, which impedes proper breathing. Again those patients in wheelchairs should at all times be aware to sit as erect as the chair allows. Perhaps a small cushion in the lumbar area may help. If we don't breathe properly, the oxygen level in the body becomes too low and the brain becomes starved of oxygen. Apart from maintaining correct posture, try to do some head and shoulder movements during the day. Tension in the neck and shoulders restricts blood supply to the brain. (see "Exercises to be done while lying in bed" part 3)

If the drowsiness is due to over-tiredness, caused by studying till late at night or driving a long distance, there are a few things you can do. Best thing would be, of course, to call it a night and go to bed! If this is not possible, park the car by the road-side and walk around the car or put your books away and take a walk around the block . Stretch, take some deep breaths, give yourself a head massage (see "Migraine" part 2), do the breathing cycle described under "Sinusitis" (part 3), drink a few glasses of fresh cold water.

Avoid drinking coffee, because, although this may seem to give you a boost for a while, a worse "low" will follow.

Try not to smoke. This will interfere with the supply of fresh air and lower the oxygen level.

Allow yourself a short relaxation or nap.

EYES

Have your eyes checked regularly. Make sure, that the glasses you wear are correct for your eyes. If you still have problems, have your blood pressure checked. See also under "Migraine" (part 2). Drink plenty of water. Practise visualisation and relaxation.

To strengthen the eye muscles and improve your eyesight, to alleviate stinging and burning sensations in the eyes, practise eye exercises. (see "Exercises to be done while lying in bed" part 3)

FEET

For healthy feet which will carry you through the day with ease, learn a foot massage and give yourself one every night. I do this instead of reading in bed before going to sleep. Lying on my back, I have one leg up in the air while working on the other foot. Keeps the legs elevated at the same time!

Wear high heels only on special occasions.

Do the foot and toe exercises included in the "Exercises to be done while lying in bed". (part 3)

If your foot problems are due to arthritis, do all the above but also read the chapter "Arthritis". (part 2)

Put your feet up as often as you can – avoid standing in one place – keep a stool handy near the kitchen bench – sit while ironing. Use your head before you use your feet! They have to carry you around for the rest of your life.

HAEMORRHOIDS, PROLAPSE OF ABDOMINAL ORGANS, VARICOSE VEINS

The tendency to varicosity of the veins and haemorrhoids is often inherited. However, even if this is the case. it does not mean that you can't do anything to avoid this problem.

Sometimes varicose veins develop during pregnancy, while childbirth can bring on haemorrhoids. Prolapse of the uterus is often a result of pregnancy too.

To avoid development of prolapse of the uterus during pregnancy, look under "Pregnancy" part 2. The pelvic tilting and the other suggestion for the strengthening of the pelvic floor are designed to avoid this problem. Practise stomach muscle strengthening exercises (see "Stomach Muscles" part 2) and stomach contractions (part 3.).

When we hear the word prolapse, we habitually think of the uterus. Women who have had a hysterectomy usually feel then that this does not concern them any longer. However, most abdominal organs can prolapse, specifically the bladder. Therefore exercising the pelvic floor is recommended practice for women and men.

To avoid developing haemorrhoids or aggravating existing ones, avoid constipation and diarrhoea (see under "Constipation" and "Diet" part 2).

Practise all inverted postures: Half Shoulderstand, Shoulderstand and Triangular Rest Pose. (see part 3) While holding these postures, draw all pelvic muscles upward and inward, tightening the sphincter muscles and then releasing them. Do this as often as you want to.

To discourage varicose veins developing and to alleviate the discomfort of existing ones, again practise all inverted postures. While holding the Half Shoulderstand, either shake the legs vigorously for several seconds at a time or make slow cycling movements with the legs. Do the last movement slowly, tensing the legs as if you are peddling up-hill.

More "do's" and "don'ts":

If overweight, try to lose weight,
Avoid alcohol and smoking tobacco,
Don't sit with the legs crossed at the knees,
Don't sit in Diamond Posture (part 3) or cross-legged position for any length of time,
When resting in bed, place the lower legs on a pillow.
Put the legs up as often as possible. Avoid standing in one spot.
Walking is a great exercise for varicose veins.

Swollen ankles too will benefit from this regimen.

HEART COMPLAINTS

Before embarking on Yoga, **please consult your doctor.**

Regular exercise strengthens the heart muscle. This strengthening process in turn slows down the heart beat over a period of time.

Why is this so? Through stronger contraction, the healthy heart pumps more blood through the circulatory system than the weak, unconditioned heart. The difference is often as much as twenty beats per minute. (from 80 to 60!)

It is easy to understand how much effort the heart is spared in a day, a month, a year...

Yoga teaches that each person is allotted a certain number of heartbeats and that therefore the person with the slow, strong heartbeat out-lives the person with the quicker, weaker heartbeat. The comparison is often drawn between a turtle and a bird. The turtle's heartbeat is considerably slower than the bird's and the turtle tends to have a much longer life span.

Pay particular attention to your breathing. Practise both the energising and the relaxing breath. (chapter 4).

Avoid physical straining and mental stress. Exercise gently and have a daily walk. All Yoga postures and movements are safe to do, but take care with the inverted postures. Monitor carefully how you experience them.

Avoid smoking – (this narrows the arteries), alcohol – (slows the blood circulation and converts to saturated fat), black coffee – (raises triglycerites (fatty substance) and cholesterol levels in the blood stream).

Have a healthy diet – see under "Diet" (part 2) for suggestions. Make sure, there is enough fibre in your diet to avoid constipation. Exclude all animal fats. Substitute fish or a vegetarian dish for meat a few times per week.

Control your weight – bring it to near or ideal level for your height and bone structure. Avoid constipation. Anxiety and stress should also be avoided.

Practise the balancing postures (part 3) as they increase the equilibrium. **Include relaxation** and **meditation** in your **daily life.**

HYPERTENSION (high blood pressure)

Quite a number of measures can be taken by the patient to minimise the severity of this disorder.

Reduce weight to on or near ideal weight for height and build. Go on a low-fat diet making sure that it contains sufficient fibre. See under "Diet" (part 2) for more indications to improve your food intake.

Gradually reduce your salt intake till it is phased out. You will enjoy your food much more, becoming aware of all the subtle flavours especially of vegetables. You will also note how "salty" other people's cooking tastes.

Drink herbal teas instead of coffee or try the very palatable coffee substitutes which are made from roasted grains, roots and berries.

Concentrate on the restoration of the natural breath as described in chapter 4. Take care not to hold the breath in. Instead concentrate on lengthening the exhalation **without straining** to do so. Remember, that the exhalation brings relaxation.

All Yoga movements and postures can safely be done except the inverted postures, the pose of a Child and pose of a Hare. Postpone these till your blood pressure is normal again.

The practise of relaxation and meditation are specifically beneficial for people with hypertension. Many of my students have successfully lowered their blood pressure that way.

INSOMNIA

Avoid tea, coffee, cocoa and cola drinks – the caffeine in these beverages inhibits sleep.
Don't go to bed before you are tired, but avoid over-tiredness.
Consider giving up smoking tobacco as nicotine is a stimulant.
Have a regular bed time – habit is helpful.
Avoid late, heavy meals – it is difficult to obtain a restful sleep when your digestive system is working at full speed.
Make sure that you are sleeping on a firm mattress and that your room is well ventilated.

Sometimes lying awake at night is due to cramps or tingling in legs and feet. If this is the case, look under "Cramps or tingling in legs and feet" (part 2)

Read about sleeping and falling asleep in chapter 5. If, after that, you still lie awake without reason, try drinking a cup of hot milk before retiring. I understand that hot milk stimulates the release by the body of a sleep-inducing substance, called tryptophan.

Whether this is true or not, Gerald's parents were convinced that this "night cap" was the secret of their sound sleeping habits. They never missed a night! Valerian tea is said to help too.

Read yourself to sleep. A good story may keep you from worrying about the problems of the day just past, or the problems expected during the day ahead.

Another suggestion: play a relaxation cassette before going to sleep.

KNEES

See under "Arthritis" and "Cramps and tingling in legs and feet" (part 2) and under "Exercises to be done while lying in bed (part 3).

MENOPAUSE

I don't have to go into specific details here as to what menopause exactly is. It will suffice to concentrate on the consequences which concern all women: cessation of menstruation and the change in hormonal flow often resulting in hot flushes.

Not every woman experiences hot flushes to the same degree. My advice is not to become agitated by them. Consider them as heat, as manifestations of energy, of Life Force even.

Don't feel as though everyone is aware of you having a hot flush. We mostly draw other people's attention to ourselves by blowing and fanning!

Remain calm – don't fan yourself – the more you move, the more heat you create. Keep the body still and just experience. Take slow deep breaths though pursed lips – this will create coolness – and sigh the breath out through a relaxed mouth. Keep this up till the flush subsides. The same routine applies during the night when the worst flushes seem to occur. Breathe this way only if you can do it without attracting attention! Otherwise just sit completely still.

Do not feel that you need a shower after every hot flush. If you bathe every day and if you are on a healthy diet, your perspiration will have no odour.

I have taken vitamin E capsules for many years now and went effortlessly through menopause, experiencing hot flushes for only three months. They probably realised that I was not going to be upset by them! Keeping a calm, relaxed attitude to the transition period is most essential. Relaxation and meditation can be a real help during this time.

MIGRAINE – HEADACHE DISTORTED VISION

If migraine or headaches occur frequently, please consult your doctor. Also have your eyes checked.

If you wake up in the morning with a headache, you may have been too warm, you may have had bad dreams, there may be insufficient ventilation in your room.

If you suffer from migraine headaches, learn to recognise the early symptoms; the impaired vision – what my doctor used to call "the bright lights". Yes, I have had years of migraines. Sometimes they were so bad, that I could not tolerate the vibrations of my own footsteps!

As soon as the first signs occur, swing into action! Sit in the Pose of a Child (part 3), your forehead on the floor. Inhale – exhale, take the buttocks off the heels while rolling onto the crown of the head, tucking the chin into the notch of the throat. Inhale – roll back onto the forehead again returning the buttocks to the heels then raise the head, while keeping the chest in touch with the thighs. Repeat this several times – stretching the throat and squeezing the neck on the inhalation; stretching the neck and squeezing the throat (thyroid glands) on the exhalation. **Don't force!**

Sit up, place your thumbs on the back of the head – on the spot where the head ends and the neck begins, just to each side of the vertebrae. There is a slight indentation under the skull. Push firmly upward and inward several times.

Give yourself a head massage. Place the fingers and thumbs on the head and make firm circular movements. There should be no sound of hair rubbing. In that case, place the fingers more firmly on the head, moving the skin over the bony structure of the skull. Make sure to cover the whole area of the head and the neck, but do not touch the vertebrae in the neck. Do all this before the migraine or headache is well and truly established. ATTACK IT IN ITS INFANCY!

After the roll, the massage and the pressure with the thumbs, have a relaxation session or take a nap.

Check whether the headache occurs more frequently after eating certain food. Some people feel, that cheese brings it on, others blame chocolate while a friend of mine can practically wait for it after eating a grapefruit. Cut down on coffee and tea and don't smoke – these constrict the blood vessels.

Don't **expect** a headache: "I hope I'll be able to come – that time of the month I usually have my headaches" or "I shouldn't be eating this – it usually brings on my headaches". Don't talk about "my" headaches – please! They are just headaches; nothing proprietary about them. Don't be possessive!

Drink plenty of fresh water – nine glasses per day. Try to get some fresh air – go walking.

Avoid boredom, worry, anxiety, stress and constipation. Know your limitations with regard to your workload. Don't overdo things – don't compare yourself with others.

Practise relaxation and meditation daily.

MULTIPLE SCLEROSIS

There are no restrictions for people with M.S. with regard to any posture or movement. As the balance is usually first affected, care should be taken when attempting standing stretches, balancing and lunging. I suggest that you stand near a wall, or put one hand against the wall and alternate hands.

For patients who are wheelchair bound it is very important to stretch on the firm surface of the floor. If this is not always possible, stretch as often as you can while sitting in the chair. Also make sure that the chair comfortably supports the spine. Experiment; place a small cushion in the lumbar area of the back. Check that your feet are resting naturally on the footrests and that the thighs are horizontal. If the knees are pushed up, place a thin piece of covered foam rubber on the seat of the chair. It is most important, that the wheelchair is **aiding** your correct posture rather than **hindering** it. If you sit slumped in the chair, your breathing will be adversely affected, which in turn will negatively affect your overall health.

The series of exercises described under "Exercises to be done while lying in bed" (part 3) are particularly suited and even more beneficial if you can lie on the floor while doing them. Once you are familiar with the movements, close your eyes and concentrate on the breathing and visualise the flow of Life Force.

If there is little or no movement in a particular limb or part of the body, keep the eyes closed and visualise the movement to take place – "see" the limb move with the breath. People have had remarkable success with consistent practice of visualisation.

M.S. patients have often considerable tension in the area of the shoulders. Fear of falling, using a walking stick or walking frame or propelling a wheelchair often induce this condition. Avoid tension setting in by frequent slow shoulder and head movements. People in wheelchairs are well advised to do the following exercise several times per day:

Inhale deeply through the nose while bringing the head and shoulders as far back as possible, arching the lumbar area of the spine – exhale bend forward toward the knees taking care not to fall out of the chair! Repeat this three times. This can be combined with the Cleansing Breath. (part 3)

Another way to practise the Cleansing Breath is to sit on the floor cross-legged. Inhale deeply through the nose while sitting up – while bending forward, exhale through the mouth – haaa. If you cannot sit cross-legged, sit on the floor, bend one knee and place the arms around the knee. Inhale through the nose – pull the knee tightly toward the chest while exhaling through the mouth – haaa., Repeat three times and change legs.

Never say "Never"! A young woman came to Ickwell Bury, the H.Q. of the Yoga for Health Foundation in England, suffering from Myositis Ossificans Progressive. This is a rare disease where the muscle turns into bone and the patient becomes like a statue. M.O.P. is classified **incurable** and **degenerative** culminating in death as even taking the slightest breath becomes an impossibility. Yet, by restoring the natural breath and practising visualisation, this girl has significantly **improved** over a time span of two and a half years.

Perhaps you too can do more with your life than you are doing at the present moment. Begin by looking at the way you breathe and make the necessary changes. (chapter 4) Start a gently exercise programme. Practise the relaxation and meditation as described in chapters 5 and 7. Also see the Healing Meditation in part 2.

OSTEOPEROSIS

There has been a great deal of publicity lately about this phenomenon. As we grow older, we are all prone to calcium loss from the bones. Particularly women after menopause are susceptible to this. In severe cases this reflects in the posture: the person develops "dowager's hump" – the neck juts forward, bringing the head out of line with the spine, while the hips and lumbar region also seem slightly forward positioned.

Ask your doctor to prescribe a calcium supplement, have a talk with your naturopath or the person in the local health-food store. It is advised to take the tablets before going to bed at night, as it is believed that the calcium loss occurs while the body is at rest.

Stretch while lying on the floor as often as possible (part 3), paying particular attention to holding the arms close to the floor, working into the shoulder area. Generally, exercise discourages calcium loss from the bones and assists in regaining lost bone density.

Include skim milk, non-fat yoghurt and cottage cheese in your diet.

Some doctors have doubts about the healing power of the mind
Some minds have doubts about the healing power of doctors!

PARKINSON'S DISEASE

People who have P.D. can improve greatly by adopting a sound Yoga practice. As there are no contra-indications for this illness, all postures and movements which the person with P.D. feels capable of doing, are perfectly safe to perform.

Walter, a very special friend of ours who was seventy one last birthday, has had P.D. for eight years. He took up Yoga some three years after the initial diagnosis when the consultant neurologist told him, that there was nothing more he could do for him than prescribing the drugs he had been on. Walter decided that any supplementary therapy was obviously up to him then and has practised Yoga daily ever since.

This same consultant neurologist gave Walter a thorough physical examination for insurance purposes last year and stated as his opinion, that Walter was fitter than most of his contemporaries who did not have P.D.! The neurologist also said in his report that he did not believe, that Walter's life expectancy was in any way affected by the disease.

Some people with P.D. take valium to cope with the cramps which are a phenomenon of the disease. Walter has relied on relaxation for this complaint and finds that it works just as well without any harmful side effects! The gently movements and postures of Yoga have also kept the stiffness at bay to a large degree.

I am telling you about Walter, because I feel that personal stories like this are inspirational.

Try to find a good Yoga teacher. There is no substitute for such a person. Also it is very beneficial to install a long mirror in the room where you exercise, so that you can observe yourself while standing and walking. This mirror can be the teacher when you are at home.

Stand in front of the mirror on the opposite side of the room – bare feet, wearing as little clothes as possible so that you can see yourself without disguise. Have a chair close by in case you need it.

Now have a good look at yourself – see yourself as if for the first time. **Don't do anything yet, just make mental notes.**

Where are your shoulders? Are they level? What about your arms? Does one seem to be longer than the other? Is this because the shoulder on that side is lower too? Are you holding the shoulders squarely or are they slumping forward? Remember, **don't do anything – just look.**

Your head, is it in the centre or are you holding it to one side like a curious child? And your face – are you frowning ? Why? Anything serious the matter?

How are your feet placed? Which way are your toes pointing? **No action – Just looking and making mental notes.**

While you are standing there, what is your breathing like? Full, slow and steady or so shallow, that it is hardly worth mentioning? Ask yourself: "What would my impression be of this person I am looking at now if this was our first meeting?"

Sit down for a moment, take a few slow deep breaths and rest. When ready, again stand in front of the mirror

Next you are consciously going to correct the way you allow your body to stand. Yes, you are reading this correctly! Surely, your body is not just standing there without you having a say in it! You are going to take charge and attend to the body's posture. If you feel the need to, you can stand against a wall.

Take some slow deep breaths – then begin with the feet. Place them apart at hip width with the feet parallel; the toes pointing straight forward. Keep the knees above the feet; don't sink through them; don't flex them back. Square your shoulders and level them; bringing one up, the other down. Now look at your arms: SAME LENGTH! Put your head in the centre, looking straight into the mirror. Don't frown – look proud!

Now look at yourself and ask the same question: "What would my impression be of this person I am looking at now if this was our first meeting?" Different? And yet, THIS IS THE SAME PERSON! However, now there is awareness.

Relax in that new posture – accept the posture – feel what it feels like so that the body will learn to "recognise" when it is holding a correct posture.

Don't tire yourself. This is enough for one session. Repeat this several times without hurrying. It is essential that you are aware of what you are doing and of what you are trying to achieve. When you are satisfied with the way you stand, you are going to progress to walking.

The walk of a person with P.D. is often more like a "shuffle" – not raising the feet and putting the heels down first. One arm is usually held close to the body and the hand on that side has an involuntary tremor. The shoulder on that side is lower, making it appear that the arm is longer. The head is to one side and inclined to the floor, probably because of fear of falling.

First we'll have to normalise the foot movement from "shuffling" to placing the heel down first followed by the toes. So, paying special attention to the feet, take one step forward putting the heel down first then rolling onto the toes while bringing the other foot's heel down, rolling onto those toes while bringing the first heel down..., etc. A good idea is, to do this "on the spot" while holding onto the back of a chair.

Exaggerate the movement till you feel you have mastered it. Say mentally: "Heel – toes... Heel – toes..." Take your time. It does not matter if you do nothing else for a few days. Heel – toes... Heel – toes... Heel – toes...

When ready for walking, stand in perfect posture at the opposite wall to the mirror, looking straight into it. Look at the floor to check that your way is clear; that there are no obstacles in your path. You are going to walk to the mirror maintaining your posture.

Begin breathing slowly and regularly. Then swing the arms rhythmically; left, right – left, right. Be aware of the movement. Say mentally: "Left, right – left, right". Then decide, that next time you say: "Left", you will put your **right** foot forward and commence walking steadily toward the mirror, swinging your arms and placing your heels to the floor first. Do not look down – remember, there is nothing on the floor.

It may seem a complicated procedure taking a long time, but this is not necessarily so. I was Walter's "mirror", giving him the instructions I have just given you and he walked perfectly normally within half an hour! This does not mean that he always did from there on – old habits are hard to break! But having done it once, he knew, that the possibility and capability were there and his walking greatly improved, even at times when he was not paying special attention to it.

Recommended postures are Cat and Cobra, twists on the floor and spinal roll – all to strengthen the spine and to keep it supple. Also stretching on the floor (part 3.) to elongate the spine and to aid the posture. Eye exercises and facial exercises as described in "Exercises to be done while lying in bed" (part 3) are recommended as are whistling and smiling!

Practise daily relaxation, visualisation and meditation.

PREGNANCY

Check that your breathing is correct – both the energising and the relaxed breath. (see chapter 4)

When going through your breathing sessions, either sit in a comfortable cross-legged position with the back straight or lie on your back on the floor (or a bed). When lying on the floor bend the knees, drawing the feet halfway toward the body. Separate the feet and let the knees fall together. Make sure that the whole of the spine is resting on the floor. If this is not the case, adjust the position of the feet so that especially the lumber is supported by the floor. The arms are by the sides, the palms of the hands are up, the eyes are gently closed.

During the first three to four months of pregnancy, stretching postures should not be practised.

From the sixth month of pregnancy it is advisable to refrain from practising the inverted postures as there is a possibility of decreasing the blood supply from the placenta to the baby.
After the fifth month it is wiser to lie on either side of the body for sleeping or relaxation in preference to lying on the back.

From seven months onward it is safer to lie on the left side to avoid compressing the vena cava inferior, the large vein which drains into the right atrium of the heart. Undue pressure on this vein can cause lowering of the blood pressure of the mother and reduced oxygen supply for the baby.

When lying on the left side, the left leg is straight, bend the right knee and place it in front of the body on the floor or bed – thigh at right angles to the body. Place a pillow under the knee and support the stomach with a cushion. The left arm is lying comfortably behind the body and the right arm is bent with the hand resting in front of the face. You may want to have a soft pillow under the head.

Before attempting the following set of exercises, **please consult your doctor and ask for his consent.** You may like to show him my suggestions.

In case there are contra indications with regard to your pregnancy, you can always **safely** practise the breathing, the foot and ankle exercises and particularly the relaxation and meditation. (see chapters 5 and 7). These will be of great value and support to you during the actual birth. Avoid constipation. (see under "Constipation").

Do the following exercises and postures at least once a day. Remember, it is the daily practice which gives you the greatest benefits.

FEET AND ANKLES: Do the exercises mentioned in the segment "Exercises to be done while lying in bed" part 3. These can also be done while sitting up.

LEGS: Sit on the floor, bend the knees, place the soles of the feet together, bring the heels close to the body, place the elbows on the inside of the knees, hold the feet or ankles: rock from side to side, while gently applying pressure to the knees with the elbows. This stretches the inner thigh muscles and firms and massages the outer thighs and the buttocks. It is advisable to do this while sitting on as firm a surface as is comfortable.

To discourage varicose veins practise the inverted positions such as Half Shoulder stand. (part 3) From the seventh month onward, or earlier if you should begin to feel uncomfortable before then, elevate the legs in the following way:

Place yourself with one side of the body alongside a wall, have a small cushion handy. Bend the knees toward the chest and, using the arms and hands, turn the body till the buttocks are touching the wall. Raise the legs along the wall and let them rest there – place the cushion under the lower back. Leave the arms by the sides with the palms of the hands upward. Close the eyes and stay there for as long as comfortable. Practise deep breathing while in this position.

Elevate the feet as often as possible. Not only to avoid varicose veins, but also to discourage swollen ankles, especially during the later stages of pregnancy. Sit down while ironing or preparing your meals – keep a stool near your work bench.

Drink plenty of water – at least nine glasses per day. (see under "Cystitis" part 2).

LEGS AND HIPS: Lie on the right side of the body, legs straight, feet together, right hand under the head, elbow on the floor, left hand in front of the body on the floor. Inhale – exhale – slowly raise the straight left leg; inhale – slowly lower the left leg to the floor while pointing the toes and keeping the knee straight. Be aware of using the muscles in the thigh and hip. Exhale.
Do this three times on each side, taking a deep breath between movements.

KNEES, THIGHS, HIPS AND PELVIS: Lunge (see part 3 of this book).

HIP AND PELVIS: Sit in Diamond Posture (part 3). Separate the feet and sit between the feet on the floor, hands in prayer position on top of the head. Inhale – raise yourself off the floor, coming onto the knees using the thigh muscles; exhale – lower yourself onto the right

heel; inhale – place the left foot 12 inches from the right knee on the floor; exhale – lower the buttocks back to the floor; inhale – rise again and return to sitting on the right heel; exhale – place left knee back to the floor; inhale – sit back between the heels on the floor; exhale – slowly lower the arms by the side.
Do this slowly both sides, concentrating on co-ordinating the movements with the breathing.

PELVIC TILTING: Lie on your back as described for breathing but this time with the knees apart, arms by the sides, palms of the hands to the floor. Inhale – arch the lumbar region of the spine, taking it off the floor while leaving the buttocks and shoulders on the floor; exhale – pull the lumbar region into the floor, pull the stomach in and tighten the sphincter muscles of the pelvic floor, drawing the vagina and anus upward and inward. TAKE AT LEAST TWO DEEP BREATHS BEFORE REPEATING THIS. Gradually build up to doing this six times, making sure that the breath has returned to normal before starting the movement again.

Another excellent pelvic floor strengthener is to "interrupt the flow" while passing urine.

SPINE: Practise the Cat, Twist and Squat as described in part 3 of the book.

Always finish your session by sitting in the Pose of a Child. (Unless you have high blood pressure of course) Adjust the Pose of a Child by opening the knees wide, keeping the toes together. Rest the forehead on the floor, leaving the arms to fall to the floor with the hands near the feet. If it presents difficulties to rest the head on the floor, please make fists of the hands, place one fist on top of the other and rest the forehead on the fists. Relax the face and let the breath flow.

Follow this by a short relaxation, being aware of your body – letting it settle – the breath relaxed. During relaxation, direct Life Force to your baby. See your baby bathing in golden Life Force.

SHRINKING AS WE GROW OLDER

We don't really shrink, although some people lose several centimetres in height. The discs between the vertebrae become thinner as we grow older, causing the spine to shorten. This often causes pinched nerves, which can be very painful.

Also our posture is not as perfect as it was in our youth, sometimes a consequence of our mental state as well.

Especially beneficial and therapeutic is stretching on the floor. When lying on the floor the spine is supported and all imbalances in the posture are negated. For stretches see part 3.

SINUSITIS

Establish what seems to cause the attack and try to avoid this trigger as much as possible. Practise special breathing cycle - see part 3.

SORE THROAT

Practise the Lion and rolling up of the tongue. (part 3) It is vital to start this as soon as the first sign of a sore throat is detected. The Lion is too dramatic to do while in company – it is not a pretty sight! However, rolling up of the tongue can be done all day as long as you don't have to talk. It is difficult to talk with your tongue rolled up in your throat!

The effect of both activities is the massaging and lubrication of the throat. Be aware of the area of the the glands in the throat; they become more pronounced. Also note the effect on the inner ear area.

Continued practice of rolling up of the tongue has been known to cure Meunier's Disease.

SPINAL PROBLEMS

If you have any doubt about the condition of your spine, please **seek advice from your doctor,** a good chiropractor or osteopath before starting on a Yoga regimen.

If your problem is due to a congenital defect or accident, find yourself a good Yoga teacher, who can give you some exercises specifically tailored to your needs.

If the spinal problem is due to arthritis, osteoperosis or Parkinson's Disease, please look under those headings in part 2.

I have had problems with my spine since I was a young woman and through a few minor accidents and one not so minor (diving into the shallow part of the swimming pool thinking it was the deep end!), I have had my share of trouble. In fact, once I was wheeled into a hospital in a wheelchair as I could no longer walk.

I am absolutely convinced that Yoga has been my salvation – without it, I am sure, I would now be a cripple.

When my spine was very bad, I found great relief from sleeping on the floor. I would lie on my back, knees bent, feet apart and drawn up toward the body – two pillows under my knees. To "cushion" the spine, use your Yoga mat to sleep on or a couple of folded-up blankets.

If you are having problems or if you are making weekly visits to your chiropractor or osteopath, consider the following routine:

Stretching lying on the floor;

Pulling head to knees;

Spinal roll;

Twist on the floor;

Cobra;

Half Locust;

Stomach contractions;

Cat;

Cat Stretch;

Squat.

Special sit-ups for spinal patients as the stomach muscles lend support to the spine.

See for all these part 3. Also pelvic tilting under "Pregnancy" part 2.

Avoid wearing high-heeled shoes.

STIFFNESS IN NECK AND SHOULDERS

If the stiffness is due to sitting in one position for an extended period, such as driving a car, sitting behind a desk or sewing machine, knitting, etc., do some head and shoulder movements. See under "Exercises to be done while lying in bed" (part 3) and under "Migraine" (part 2).

Do not roll the head around. This should definitely be discouraged as it can be quite hazardous, due to the delicate nature of the vertebrae in the neck.

If the stiffness is due to arthritis, look under "Arthritis". (part 2).

STOMACH MUSCLES – (strengthening of)

When we speak about stomach muscles, we usually mean abdominal muscles and not just the muscles in the area of the stomach. In this chapter I am discussing the abdominal muscles but I will use both terms in order to create a little more variety in the text.

It is very important to have strong abdominal muscles. Not only for aesthetic reasons – indeed, it looks so much better but for plain health reasons as well. The internal and external abdominal muscles support the abdominal organs as well as the spine.

Restoration of the natural breath will go a long way in improving the tone of the stomach muscles. (see chapter 4) Be aware, that through taking tranquilisers the abdominal muscles often become spongy. Tranquilisers not only relax the mind, but the body is directly influenced.

Do some stomach muscle strengthening exercises as soon after childbirth as possible – don't let them settle!

Try leg-raising:

Lie flat on the floor, arms by the sides with the palms of the hands to the floor:
Inhale – exhale – raise the straight left leg as high as you can;
Inhale – lower the straight left leg slowly to the floor; exhale.
Take a deep breath in and out. Repeat this with the right leg.

It is important to do this **slowly** and to **co-ordinate** the **movement** with the **breath.**

When you can do this comfortably, try both legs:
Inhale – exhale – **pull the small of the back into the floor** and raise both straight legs, **holding the small of the back tightly to the floor;** inhale – lower the legs slowly to the floor, again **keeping the spine to the floor;** exhale.

It is important to keep the lumbar region of the spine to the floor while raising and lowering the legs. If you cannot manage this, please **do not** attempt the raising of both legs. Wait till the stomach muscles have improved. There is too much strain on the spine when the lumbar vertebrae arch off the floor.

A very simple and effective thing to do is tightening the stomach muscles. This can be done standing, sitting or lying down. Inhale – and on the exhalation tighten the stomach muscles by pulling the stomach upward and inward. Relax and take a deep breath in and out before repeating.

STOMACH MUSCLE STRENGTHENERS

When starting on a regimen of strengthening the abdominal muscles, begin with the ones numbered 1 and 2. These are completely safe to perform with any spinal condition and particularly number 1 will strengthen the abdominal muscles without any strain on the spine. When you find yourself comfortable with these, progress to number 3, 4 and 5. Monitor carefully, that you are able to come into a sitting position **keeping the spine aligned.** If you have to use the elbows or if the feet tend to come off the floor, go back to numbers 1 and 2 till the stomach muscles are stronger.

1a – Lie on the back on the floor, arms by the sides, palms down, feet together. Arms and hands remain relaxed in 1a and 1b. Inhale – exhale, raise the head **only**, keeping the shoulders to the floor, feel the tightening of the muscles very low in the abdomen when raising the head; inhale – lower the head to the floor; exhale. Repeat two times. Then take a deep breath in and out.

1b – Same position: Inhale – exhale, raise the head and shoulders off the floor, keeping the lower tips of the shoulder blades to the floor, feel the area below the navel tightening when raising head and shoulders; inhale – slowly lower the shoulders and head to the floor; exhale. Repeat two times. Then take a deep breath in and out.

1c – Same position: Inhale – exhale, raise the head, shoulders and shoulderblades off the floor, **keeping the lumbar region on the floor,** stretching the hands toward the feet, feel the whole abdomen and the area between the floating ribs tighten when raising head, shoulders and shoulder blades; inhale – collapse the body to the floor; exhale. Take a few slow deep breaths then repeat.

Relax while deep breathing, sending Life Force to the abdominal area.

2.– Lie on the back on the floor, hands behind the small of the back, palms to the floor, feet together.

Inhale – raise the head as if looking at the toes; exhale, using pressure of the hands only as much as needed, slowly sit up; place the hands on the thighs – inhale – keeping the chin toward the chest, the spine rounded, slowly "unroll" the body to the floor; exhale when on the floor; take a deep breath in and out. Repeat three times. Then relax, deep breathing, sending Life Force to the abdominal area.

3.– Lie on the back on the floor, arms along the front of the body, palms on the thighs, feet together.

Inhale – raise your head; exhale, slowly come into a sitting position; inhale – chin toward the chest, spine rounded, sliding the hands along the front of the body, slowly "unroll" the body to the floor; exhale when on the floor; take a deep breath in and out. Repeat three times. Then relax, deep breathing, sending Life Force to the abdominal area.

4.– Same position as above, but now hold the elbows with the hands, keeping the arms close to the body throughout.
Inhale – raise your head; exhale, slowly come into a sitting position; inhale – chin toward the chest, spine rounded, slowly "unroll" the body to the floor; exhale when on the floor; take a deep breath in and out. Repeat three times. Then relax, deep breathing, sending Life Force to the abdominal area.

5.– Same position as above, but now place the hands behind the neck. Inhale – raise your head; exhale, slowly come into a sitting position; inhale – keeping the elbows out sideways, head forward, spine rounded, slowly "unroll" the body to the floor; exhale when on the floor; take a deep breath in and out. Repeat three times. Then relax, deep breathing, sending Life Force to the abdominal area.

Also practise "stomach contractions" part 3.

STROKE

If you have had a stroke, you should start to do some gentle movement as soon as possible so that rehabilitation can begin. The "Exercises to be done while lying in bed" (part 3) are excellent for this purpose.

Find a good remedial Yoga teacher who can give you exercises to suit your particular need.

Restore the natural breath (see chapter 4). **This is most important.**

Consider improving your diet (see under "Diet" and "Heart complaints" part 2). Give up smoking.

Meditation is recommended and especially the healing meditation (part 2) will be of great value.

VITAMINS

There are two schools of thought regarding the taking of vitamin supplements. One says that if you are on a balanced diet and eat a little of all necessary food components, you should not need to take any.

The other school of thought maintains that there is no such thing as a balanced diet in this modern age we live in. With the phenomena of impoverished soil, chemical fertilisers and insecticides most foods have lost much of their nutritional qualities. Adherents to this school of thought say that we virtually would have to consume a bucketful of food each day in order to receive all minerals and vitamins needed for growth or maintenance of health.

They further point to the effects of pasteurising, homogenising, freezing, the waxing and gassing of certain fruits, conservatives, food additives as well as hormones and antibiotics fed to cattle and fowl.

The latest development in interfering with the quality of our food supply is the proposal to introduce irradiation. As it is not too late to become involved at the time of this book going to print, it is important, that people concerned with the integrity of food available to the community, seek information regarding this matter and, if they share my concern, try to find ways and means to exert pressure on the government to stop this development.

The people who are in favour of taking vitamin supplements also consider the influence of environmental pollution (noise and air) and personal pollution (smoking, taking the birth control pill, wearing a birth control device).

They advocate that women after menopause should take vitamin E to offset the effects of reduced oestrogen production and calcium to discourage osteoperosis, to which this group is particularly prone.

I adhere to the second school and have taken the whole alphabet for years. Well, not quite the whole alphabet, but near enough! I dont like eating large amounts of food and feel, that it would indeed be difficult to eat a little of everything needed each day.

The decision is yours! Seek advice from a good naturopath; he has made a thorough study of the subject.

WATER

The importance of drinking water has been mentioned many times in this book, so perhaps it does not warrant a special heading. However, just because it is so vital, I would like to repeat: Please try to drink at least nine glasses of water each day starting first thing in the morning. (see "Early morning routine" part 2)

Drinking other fluids such as fruit juice, coffee and tea does not have the same effect. Coffee and tea are drugs and fruit juice, while healthy if fresh, has a certain amount of sugar in it and hence, consuming large quantities of it has its draw-backs. Only fresh water has this unique quality of flushing the body system through.

WEIGHT REDUCTION

Don't experiment with all kinds of diets. One-sided diets such as grapefruit, egg, banana or carbohydrate diets are hard to keep, simply because they are boring. There is nothing like boredom to make you want to eat more!

Besides, they are unbalanced and hence unhealthy and sometimes even downright dangerous. Especially teenagers, whose bodies are still developing, can do untold damage to themselves with such regimen.

That kind of diet often results in nervous tension, depression, dull skin and lack-lustre hair as well as lack of energy. The extreme diets also place us outside society as it becomes difficult to mix socially.

Best strategy is to eat **a little of all foods.** Don't overeat – use a small plate. At mealtimes put the food you allow yourself on the plate and do not go back for seconds. Eat slowly, chewing well.
Don't eat between meals.

To stave off hunger pangs, have some "safe foods" handy: raw carrots (slice or grate them if your teeth complain), slices of cucumber, sticks of celery, capsicum, raw cauliflower, aniseed.

When you are losing weight, exercise to tone the muscles and skin and to accelerate the reducing process.

Keep busy – idle hands and minds will invite thoughts of food if you are so inclined.

Watch out for establishing habits such as eating while reading or while watching T.V. – if you must eat, have some of your "safe food".

If you feel the urge to eat come on, go for a walk around the block, phone a friend, do some weeding – anything to divert your train of thought.

During relaxation and meditation, visualise the goal you want to achieve – see yourself as you would like to be.

Read chapter 6 and see "Diet", "Constipation" and "Water" (part 2).

ALTERNATE NOSTRIL BREATHING

Sit in a comfortable cross-legged position – spine erect – head aligned with the spine – eyes closed – left hand on the left knee with the forefinger and thumb touching. This hand gesture is called Jnana Mudra – the forefinger represents the spirit of Self – the thumb represents the spirit of the Universe – the circle created by placing the two together signifies the Infinite or infinity.

Place the right thumb on the right side of the nose – the two first fingers in the centre of the forehead – the ring finger on the left side of the nose. Close the right nostril with the thumb – breathe in through the left nostril – close the nostril with the ring finger – open the right nostril – breathe out through the right nostril. Hold the same finger posture – breathe in through the right nostril – close the nostril with the thumb – open the left nostril – breathe out through the left nostril. Keeping the eyes closed – place the right hand on the right knee. This is one round.

Practise at least three rounds – concentrating on calming the mind, clearing the air passages and balancing the energy flow in the body.

This is very beneficial in times of stress and for people with high blood pressure. In case of high blood pressure do NOT hold the inhalation, but concentrate on the exhalation.

BALANCING POSTURES

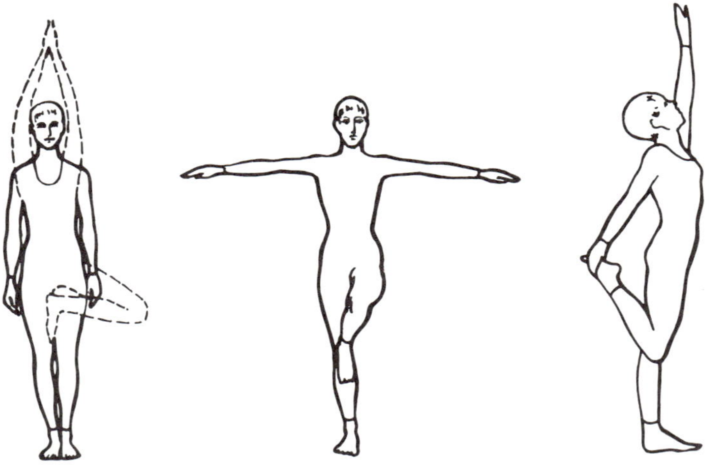

Balancing improves our posture, improves the balance and increases our equilibrium. When going into a balancing posture, focus the eyes on a spot straight ahead at eye level or on a spot on the floor, taking care not to bend the neck.

Stand quietly on both feet - focus the eyes – bring the weight over on one foot and gently go into the posture.

While in the posture, keep the breath flowing rhythmically, hold the focus and imagine to be a large tree with roots growing from your foot through the floor deep into the soil beneath – you are growing toward the sky – so gently stretch while in the posture.

When in the posture with the arms out at shoulder level, imagine to breathe in through the finger tips into the thymus gland in the centre of the chest. Hold the Life Force there – see the area begin to glow – breathe out through the finger tips again.

The thymus gland is understood to be involved with the functioning of our immune system and the energy level in the body.

BREATHING PRACTICE TO DISCOURAGE CHEST COLDS AND COUGHS

Ideally the following breathing cycles are practised early in the morning when the air is clean – outside or near an open window. Sometimes it is wiser to practise in a well-ventilated room as it can be harmful to breathe in air which is too cold.

Sit in a comfortable cross-legged position – spine erect – the head aligned with the spine.

We are going to use the hands to tap, pat and rub the chest. Take care to relax the wrists so that the hands are kind as they touch the ribcage.

Inhale deeply through the nose – hold the breath – tap the top of the chest lightly with the finger tips – exhale through the mouth with a "haaaa" sound while bending forward toward the floor – inhale vigorously through the nose while returning to sitting position – exhale calmly through the nose. Repeat two times.

Then sit quietly with the eyes closed – breathing slowly through the nose.

Bend the fingers back, flattening the palms of the hands – inhale deeply through the nose – hold the breath – vigorously rub the lower part of the chest with the flat part of the hands – exhale through the mouth with a "haaaa" sound while bending forward toward the floor – inhale vigorously through the nose while returning to a sitting position – exhale calmly through the nose. Repeat two times.

Again sit quietly with the eyes closed – breathing slowly through the nose.

"Cup" the hands by closing the fingers and bending the hands inward. There should be a hollow sound when the hands fall to the ribcage – not a slapping sound which would occur if the flat of the hands patted the chest. It is the air which should cause the vibration in the chest. Make sure to relax the wrists. Take care that the hands do not touch the soft area of the stomach between the floating ribs.

Inhale deeply through the nose – hold the breath – pat the lower part of the chest with the "cupped" hands – exhale through the mouth with a "haaaa" sound while bending forward toward the floor – inhale vigorously through the nose while returning to a sitting position – exhale calmly through the nose. Repeat two times.

Sit quietly with the eyes closed – breathing slowly through the nose.

Make loose fists – inhale deeply through the nose – bend the body slightly forward – let the head relax – let the soft fists fall to the ribcage at the back wherever you can reach – exhale through the mouth with a "haaaa" sound while bending forward toward the floor – inhale vigorously through the nose while returning to a sitting position – breathe out calmly through the nose. Repeat two times.

Caution: Do NOT let the fists fall below the ribcage so that they hit the area of the kidneys.

Lie on the back – the knees bent – the feet drawn up toward the body – feet apart – knees falling together – arms by the sides – palms of the hands turned upward. Breathe slowly and rhymically, letting the body settle. Be aware of Life Force in the whole area of the chest.

BREATHING TECHNIQUE TO ALLEVIATE THE EFFECTS OF HEAD COLDS AND SINUSITIS

Sit in a comfortable cross-legged position, hands resting on the knees or in Diamond Posture (part 3) with the hands resting on the thighs. Spine is erect, the head aligned with the spine.

The breathing technique described here is called Kapalabhati and is an excellent method of clearing the air passages and the head.

Breathing is through the nose only. The chest is slightly extended and held still; the movement is solely in the abdomen.

The inhalation is passive, occurring through relaxing the abdominal wall, allowing it to come forward. The exhalation is dynamic, caused by pulling the abdomen sharply inward, making a sound as if blowing the nose.

The inhalation is about three times the duration of the exhalation which is short and sharp. To check whether the movement is indeed correct – place the palm of one hand on the abdomen and feel the movement – outward on the inhalation, inward on the exhalation.

Begin by doing it slowly, gradually building up the tempo. Have a few short sessions with rests in between. Do not become afraid if dizziness is experienced. This is no cause for concern as it is only due to an unusually generous supply of oxygen to the area of the head.

After the session, lie on the back with the knees drawn up – the feet apart – the knees falling together – arms and hands relaxed. Let the breathing, the heart beat and the whole body settle. Visualise the Life Force in the head, the nasal passages and the sinuses.

This is also great therapy when drowsy or sleepy while wanting or having to stay awake. It will clear the head thoroughly.

CAUTION: People with heart conditions or lung disease should NOT practise Kapalabhati.

CAMEL POSTURE

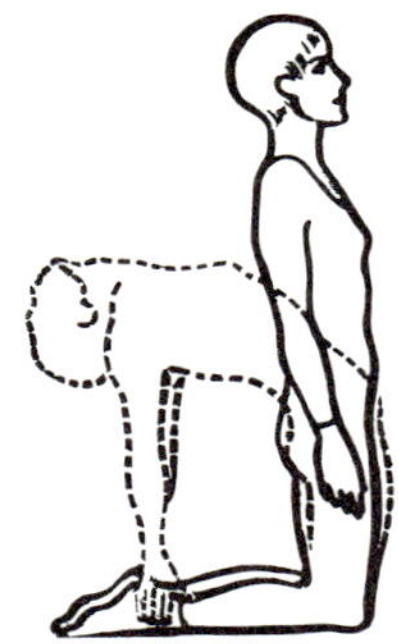

Kneel down on both knees – knees at hip width – feet same distance apart. Inhale – gently hang the head back – arms and hands behind the body. Move the whole body backwards so that the hands can hold the heels. When the hands are in touch with the heels, push the hips and thighs forward. Deep breathing in this position.

When coming out of this posture – take care. First bring the head forward. Inhale – leading with the head, return to starting position. Exhale. Relax in the Pose of a Child, feeling Life Force flowing into the area where you feel most affected by the posture.

Simple CAMEL POSTURE

If you cannot reach the heels with the hands, modify the posture. Kneel down on both knees, place the palms of the hands on the back below the waist – fingers pointing to the floor. Inhale – gently hang the head back and bend backwards while pushing the hips and thighs forward with the hands.

Hold this posture while breathing deeply. Returning to starting position is the same as for the Camel Posture.

CAT POSTURE

The Cat is essentially a matter of hollowing and arching the spine. To make this into a remedial movement it has to be executed **slowly**, with awareness and visualising the spine as it moves. The arching and hollowing both start at the lowest vertebra and ends at the top vertebra which is situated in the head. **Elbows remain straight throughout.**

Kneel down, place the palms of the hands on the floor – hands directly below the shoulders, knees slightly apart, directly below the hips. Exhale – inhale – begin hollowing the lower spine; the middle part, the area between the shoulder blades, then raise the head; exhale – begin arching: pull the tail under, pull the stomach in, arch between the shoulderblades, then the head comes down and inward toward the knees. When in this position, all muscles are tight: thigh muscles, abdominal muscles and the muscles of the pelvic floor. Repeat this movement at least three times. Lie down to rest with the knees drawn up toward the body, the feet apart on the floor, the knees falling together, arms and hands relaxed. Take deep breaths, sending Life Force to the spine.

CAT STRETCH

Same starting position as for the Cat posture. Hold the position of the thighs and buttocks – **do not alter it.** Inhale – slide the hands forward at the same time lowering the chest and chin toward the floor. Hold the position – breathe deeply and "sink" the chest further toward the floor with each exhalation – accept the posture.

Rest in the Pose of a Child – breathe gently – sending Life Force to the place where you feel most affected by the posture.

This posture is very beneficial for the spine, for the shoulders and upper arms.

POSE OF A CHILD

Kneel down – knees and feet together – sit on the heels. Staying on the heels, place the forehead to the floor. The hands are on the floor near the feet – then relax the arms, letting the elbows and shoulders fall toward the floor. Deep breathing – awareness is in the area of the third eye or in the area of the pineal gland – send the Life Force there.

In case of high blood pressure, modify the posture by making fists of both hands – placing one fist on top of the other in front of the body on the floor and resting the forehead on top of the fists. Carefully monitor whether this posture is beneficial for you.

CLEANSING BREATH

Standing: Standing upright with the feet wide apart – arms by the sides. Inhale through the nose – raise the arms sideways and upward – stretch tall holding the breath – Exhale through the mouth with a sharp "haaaa" sound – bend forward, dropping the arms and hands toward the floor. Stay there till there is no air in the lungs left. Inhale through the nose – come up into a standing position, raising the arms outward and upward. Repeat at least three times.

If the spine is weak, a sitting position may be preferred.

Sitting 1: Sit with the right leg straight forward – the left leg bent – arms loosely around the knee. Inhale through the nose – raise the head – open the chest – Exhale through the mouth with a sharp "haaaa" sound – bring the head toward the knee simultaneously pulling the knee tightly toward the chest. Repeat three times. Change legs.

Sitting 2: Sit cross-legged – hands holding the feet. Inhale through the nose – Exhale through the mouth with a sharp "haaaa" sound – bend forward – bringing the head toward the floor – Inhale return to sitting position. Repeat at least three times.

Sitting 3: Sit cross-legged – hands holding the feet – chin toward the chest – head toward the floor – the spine is rounded. Exhale through the mouth with a sharp "haaaa" sound – Inhale through the nose – roll over as in Spinal Roll (part 3) – Exhale through the mouth "haaaa" while rolling forward again. Repeat at least three times.

Take care not to let the buttocks leave the floor while rolling forward, thereby losing control over the movement.

Mother is relaxing in the Cobra

COBRA POSTURE

Lie on the stomach on the floor – palms of the hands just below the shoulders on the floor, elbows close to the body, forehead to the floor, toes touching. Keep the legs relaxed throughout. While moving, the awareness is in the throat where the thyroid and para-thyroid glands are located and in the chest where the thymus gland is.
Exhale – inhale – raise the head, the shoulders and chest off the floor. Keeping the shoulders low, do not straighten the elbows, keep the hips and thighs on the floor; exhale; return the chest, shoulders and chin to the floor, then the forehead. Repeat two times.

Rest by placing the right cheek to the floor, arms alongside the body, elbows slightly bent, palms up, feet apart, heels falling inward or outward. Deep breathing, directing Life Force to the kidneys and adrenal glands.

DIAMOND POSTURE

Kneel down – knees and feet together – sit on the heels, rest the hands on the front of the thighs. This is Diamond Posture. If this presents difficulties for the knees, modify the posture by placing a small cushion or rolled-up towel on the calves and by sitting on the cushion or towel. This will take the strain off the knees.

EXERCISES TO BE DONE WHILE LYING IN BED – early morning or when unwell.

Although usually Yoga is practised on the floor, preferably carpetted or using a Yoga mat, there are situations when this is impossible. Either you are unwell, perhaps even hospitalised, or there is not enough space in the bedroom to allow exercising while there is no alternative space in the dwelling available either.

Please go to the bathroom before beginning the following exercises. You cannot practise deep breathing with a full bladder. While in the bathroom, clean your tongue, (see "Early morning routine" – part 2), rinse your mouth and gargle with luke-warm water. Finish by drinking a large glass of water (luke warm in summer, warm in winter).

Go back to bed! Do all the following exercises slowly and in conjunction with the breath. If possible, repeat every movement two or three times. The repetition is important but will obviously depend on your condition and the time you have available.

Send Life Force to each part of the body as you are working on it, using the mind to direct the Cosmic Energy to that particular body part.

Use the energising breath – expand the ribcage on the inhalation, contract the ribcage on the exhalation; hold the abdomen still and controlled. Make sure to take a few slow deep breaths between each section.

Begin by stretching: Inhale – bring the arms overhead pushing the toes down, stretch – on the exhalation let the arms fall by the sides. Repeat three times.

If stretching in bed presents difficulties because the hands are touching the bed head or the wall overhead, bend the arms and hold the elbows – keep the upper arms and elbows in touch with the bed and stretch from the elbows rather than from the hands. Another solution is to lie upside down on the bed – head at the foot end!

TOES: Hold the feet at right angles to the bed. Inhale – push only the toes toward the bed; pull only the toes toward the head; exhale. Repeat three times.

Inhale – separate the toes; close the toes; exhale. Repeat three times.

FEET: Inhale – push both feet toward the bed; pull both feet toward the head; exhale. Repeat three times.

Point the feet toward the bed: Inhale – push the outside of the feet toward the bed; push the inside of the feet toward the bed; exhale. Repeat three times.

Pull the toes toward the head: Inhale – keeping the toes flexed, push the outside of the feet toward the bed; push the inside of the feet toward the bed; exhale. Repeat three times.

ANKLES: Inhale – rotate the feet clockwise; exhale. Repeat three times.

Inhale – rotate the feet anti-clockwise; exhale. Repeat three times.

KNEES: Keep the foot in touch with the bed right through: Inhale – exhale – bend one knee, sliding the foot toward the body bring the heel close to the buttocks; inhale – keeping the foot flexed, slide the foot back to starting position, stretch the leg; exhale. Same with the other leg. Repeat two times.

Bend the knees put the soles of the feet together: Inhale – exhale – slide the heels close to the buttocks;

inhale – straighten the legs along the surface of the bed, trying to keep the soles of the feet together; exhale. Repeat three times.

HANDS: Inhale – make fists by bringing one finger at a time to the palm of each hand, start by the thumb; exhale – clench the fists tightly; inhale – open the hands one finger at a time, starting with the little finger; exhale – spread and stretch the fingers as wide as possible. Relax the hands. Repeat two times.

Same as above but now starting to close the hands, begin with the little fingers and opening, begin with the thumbs. Repeat two times.

WRISTS: Make loose fists: Inhale – move hands up, move hands down using the wrists; exhale. Repeat three times.

Loose fists: Inhale – move hands to the right then to the left, bending at the wrists; exhale. Repeat three times.

Loose fists: Inhale – rotate the hands clockwise; exhale. Repeat three times.

Loose fists: Inhale – rotate the hands anti-clockwise; exhale. Repeat three times.

ARMS: Inhale – arms out sideways at shoulder level, hands loose fists; exhale – bend the arms as if there is resistance, bring the fists to the shoulders; inhale – open the hands, stretch the arms as wide as possible; exhale – relax the arms. Repeat three times.

Put the palms of the hands together, place the hands in prayer position on the chest. Inhale – press palms of the hands together; exhale; relax. Repeat three times.

TORSO: Inhale – clench the muscles in the buttocks and thighs as tightly as possible; exhale – relax. Repeat three times.

Inhale – lift the buttocks off the bed; exhale – slowly return to the bed. When there is no air left, push the small of the back into the bed, pull the stomach in, tense the muscles in the thighs and buttocks while pulling the sphincter muscles in the pelvic floor upward and inward. Do this as long as you can, holding the breath out; then take a deep breath in and relax. Repeat this three times **making sure that the breath is normal again before starting a new round.**

Bend one knee, hold it with both hands close to the chest. Inhale – exhale – pull the stomach in, bring the head toward the knee; inhale – return the head to the bed; exhale. Repeat three times. Same with other leg. Then with both legs. Three times.

SHOULDERS: Inhale – extend the chest, push the shoulders hard into the bed; exhale – keeping the head on the bed, pull the shoulders toward each other squeezing the chest; inhale – return the shoulders to the bed; exhale. Repeat three times.

Same as above, but this time raise the head as well as the shoulders off the bed on the exhalation. Repeat three times.

Inhale – raise the shoulders high toward the ears; exhale – push the shoulders as far down as possible. Repeat three times.

Inhale – rotate the shoulders forward; exhale. Repeat three times.

Inhale – rotate the shoulders backward; exhale. Repeat three times.

NECK: Place the head in the centre. Inhale – exhale – turn the head bring the right ear and cheek to the bed; inhale – return to centre; exhale, turn the head bring the left ear and cheek to the bed; inhale – return to centre; exhale. Repeat three times.

Inhale – exhale – pull the chin forward into the notch in the throat; inhale – arch the neck, place the top of the head on the bed, pushing the chin upward; exhale – return to starting position. Repeat two times.

THROAT: Inhale – roll the tongue up inside the mouth till the tip of the tongue is touching the throat; hold as long as possible; exhale, relax. Repeat three times.

FACE: Inhale – drop the lower jaw as far as possible; exhale – close the mouth. Repeat three times.

Slightly open the mouth: Inhale – push the lower jaw to the right then to the left; exhale. Repeat three times.

Inhale – pull the lower lip over the upper lip toward the nose; exhale – pull the upper lip over the lower lip toward the chin. Repeat three times.

Inhale – blow up both cheeks; hold; exhale. Repeat three times.

Inhale – blow up one cheek; hold the breath, push the air from one cheek to the other; exhale. Repeat three times.

Inhale – say silently: aaah, eeeh, uuuh, using exaggerated lip movements; exhale. Repeat three times.

EYES: Keeping the head in the centre throughout:

Inhale – Look up, look down; two times; exhale, close the eyes.

Inhale – look right, look left; two times; exhale, close the eyes.

Inhale – looking diagonally across: left corner up, right corner down; two times; exhale, close the eyes.

Inhale – right corner up, left corner down; two times; exhale, close the eyes.

Inhale – look far away, look to the tip of the nose; two times, exhale; close the eyes.

Inhale – open the eyes as wide as possible, blink as hard as possible; two times; exhale, close the eyes.

Inhale – slowly rotate the eyes clockwise; exhale, close the eyes.

Inhale – slowly rotate the eyes anti-clockwise; exhale, close the eyes.

Place the palms of the hands over the closed eyes, not touching the eyelids – exclude all light; Inhale – hold the breath and imagine the eyes to be two deep, cool pools of water; exhale, take the hands away keeping the eyes closed.

Vigorously rub the palms of the hands together – feel the heat being generated; place the palms of the hands over the closed eyes not touching the eyelids; exclude all light; open the eyes and imagine that with each deep inhalation, Life Force is flowing from the hands into the eyes. Take several deep breaths; close the eyes before taking the hands away on an exhalation. Open the eyes looking down first.

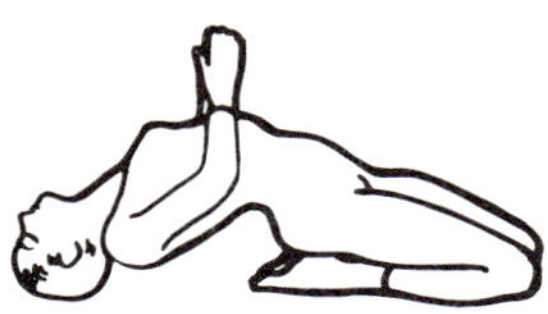

FISH POSTURE

Sit in Diamond Posture (part 3) Open the feet wide enough to enable you to sit between the feet on the floor, if possible keep the knees together. Place the hands on the soles of the feet, fingertips on the heels. Hanging the head back, lower yourself onto the right elbow then onto the left, going further back till the crown of the head is on the floor. Place the hands in prayer position on the chest. Keep the shoulders well back, arch the spine, open the chest. Breathe deeply in this position, visualising Life Force to stream into the chest.

When coming out of this posture, place the hands back on the feet, raise the head and, using the elbows, slowly return to a sitting position. Bring the legs out forward and give them a shake. Relax in the Pose of a Child, breathe slowly, sending Life Force to the spine.

Simple Fish Posture

Lie on the back on the floor, feet together. Now recline onto the elbows, forearms and palms of the hands on the floor. Hang the head back, slide the elbows toward the feet till the crown of the head is on the floor. If you feel comfortable in this position, place the hands in prayer position on the chest. Breathe deeply, visualising Life Force to stream into the chest. If it feels as if the neck is not strong enough to maintain this posture, please stay on the elbows, keeping the shoulders back, so that the chest is "open".

When coming out of the posture: using the elbows, inhale – raise the head as if looking at the toes; exhale, lower the head to the floor; take a deep breath in and out. Relax by hugging the knees to the chest and rolling. (see ROLLS part 3) Breathe slowly, sending Life Force to the spine.

HALF LOCUST POSTURE

Lie on the stomach on the floor – feet together – right cheek to the floor – arms beneath the body – palms of the hands touching the front of the thighs.
Inhale – exhale – raise the left leg, keep the hand on the floor; inhale – stretch the leg upward and away from the body; exhale – slowly lower the leg to the floor. Take a deep breath in and out.
Place the left cheek on the floor and repeat, raising the right leg. Relax and direct Life Force to the kidneys and adrenal glands.

HALF SHOULDER STAND

Lie on the back on the floor – feet together – arms by the sides – palms of the hands on the floor.
Inhale – pull the small of the back into floor; exhale – raise both legs, then the hips off the floor and rest the hips in the hands – the legs slightly tilted toward the head. Hold this posture for as long as it is comfortable – eyes closed – breathing rhythmically – visualising Life Force to flow to the area of the heart or the area where you feel most in need.

Coming down: Lower the legs overhead toward the floor, tucking the chin tightly into the notch in the throat, return the hands to the floor as in starting position. (This is the Plough Posture). Inhale – slowly roll the spine to the floor, keeping the legs close to the torso; exhale when the spine is on the floor and the toes are pointing to the ceiling; inhale – KEEPING THE SMALL OF THE BACK ON THE FLOOR, slowly lower the straight legs to the floor. Exhale.

If, while lowering the legs to the floor the small of the back begins to arch, bend the knees and return the legs to the floor that way. Do NOT lower the straight legs while the lower spine is arched off the floor – this puts too much strain on the spine.

Not suitable for people with high blood pressure.

POSE OF A HARE

Assume the Pose of a Child – do not move the position of the head – take the buttocks off the heels and roll over onto the crown of the head. Breathe slowly and deeply – awareness in the pituitary gland.

In case of high blood pressure do NOT practise the Pose of a Hare.

HEAD TO KNEE POSE lying on the back

Lie on the back – arms by the sides – legs together. Inhale – exhale – raise the right leg – bend the knee and hug the knee toward the chest.

Inhale – exhale – raise the head and bring the head toward the knee – tightly pull the abdomen in, breathing out completely; inhale – return the head to the floor; exhale. Repeat three times. Return the leg to the floor on an inhalation; exhale.

Take a few slow deep breaths before making the movement with the left leg.

Then make the same movement with both legs bent and held toward the chest.

When finished, lie quietly on the back – breathe deeply and send Life Force to the place in the body where the need is greatest.

Benefits the digestion – discourages constipation – wonderful therapy to alleviate a feeling of tightness and discomfort in the lower back as it relaxes the muscles running parallel to the spine and those attached to each vertebra. Take care to breathe OUT when taking the head toward the knee(s).

Caution: People with high blood pressure are not advised to practise this movement.

LION POSE and ROLLING UP of the TONGUE

Sit in Diamond Posture – spine erect – head aligned with the spine – hands on the thighs with the fingers spread. Inhale – exhale – open the mouth wide and put the tongue out as far as possible – open the eyes wide – stiffen the whole body. Hold till the need for inhaling occurs. Relax the face and take a few deep breaths before repeating.

To alleviate sore throats and to discourage sore throats developing, practise this pose outside in the early morning sun. Face the sun – KEEPING THE EYES CLOSED – tilt the head slightly back so that the warmth of the sun is felt in the mouth and throat while practising the Lion Pose.

A far less spectacular practice which can be executed quite unobtrusively and has excellent results is the following: Roll the tongue up in the closed mouth till the tip of the tongue is touching the back of the throat past the soft palate. Hold this posture while breathing slowly and rhythmically, visualising Life Force to bathe the throat.

Be aware how pronounced the glands in the throat become while holding the posture – feel what happens inside the ears and notice that the throat is lubricated.

This practice has been known to have a very positive effect on Meunier's Disease. In that case visualisation should be directed to the inner ear.

LUNGE

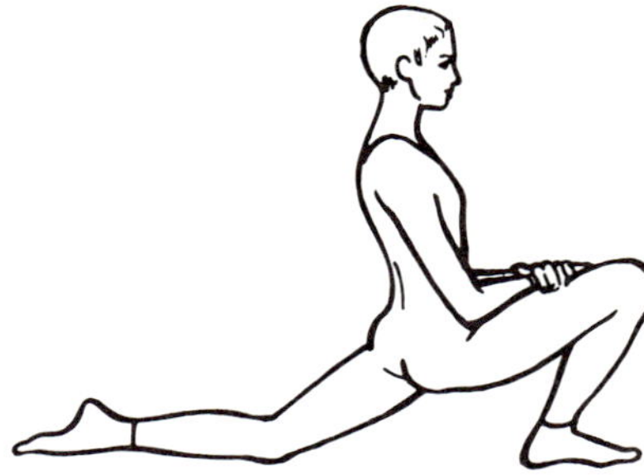

Kneel down on the right knee – left foot forward on the floor – the foot is slightly forward from the left knee – hands on the knee. Inhale – exhale – lunge forward, keep the left heel on the floor, lower the pelvis to the floor, holding the trunk and head upright. Take a few breaths in this position, sinking into the lunge. Inhale – return to starting position – exhale. Relax – feel Life Force stream into the area most affected by this posture.

Variations for hands positions: Hands in prayer position on the chest or arms by the sides – fingers pointing to the floor.

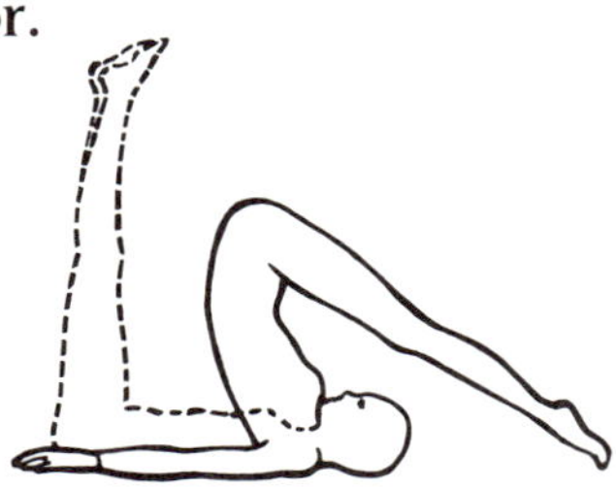

PLOUGH POSTURE

Same beginning as Half Shoulder Stand. Instead of bringing the legs up to near vertical, bring the feet overhead on the floor – tucking the chin tightly into the notch in the throat – arms and hands remain on the floor throughout. Keep the breath flowing rhythmically, direct Life Force to the spine, thyroid and para thyroid glands.

Coming out of the posture is the same as for the Half Shoulder Stand.

Not suitable for people with high blood pressure

RELAXATION POSE

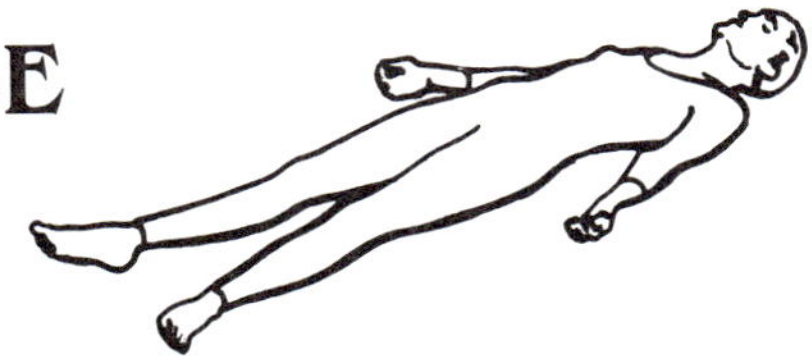

Lie on the back on the floor – body in a straight line – head in line with the spine – chin toward the chest – shoulders low and relaxed toward the floor – palms of the hands turned upward – feet twelve to eighteen inches apart – toes falling outward.

If it is uncomfortable to lie flat on the back because of spinal problems – place a pillow under the bent knees – this will "flatten" the spine and alleviate tension in the lumbar region.

If the head tends to fall back thereby arching the back of the neck and straining the throat – place a small cushion under the back of the head.

ROLLS

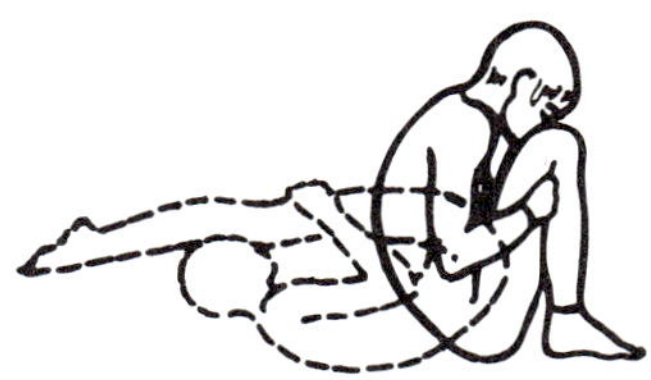

SPINAL ROLL: This can be combined with the Cleansing Breath. Breathe in through the nose and breathe out through the mouth with a sharp "haaaa" sound.
Sit with the knees drawn up to the chest, hands behind the knees, head toward the knees, spine rounded. Hold the spine in that position throughout.
Exhale "haaaa": inhale – roll overhead, straightening the legs; exhale "haaaa", bending the knees, roll forward again to starting position. Repeat this as often

as you like. Make it a relaxing movement – no pushing or forcing, letting the spine become more and more flexible.

Then lie down; take deep breaths letting the breath settle back to normal and the heart beat become slow and steady. Direct Life Force to the whole spine.

HEAD ROLL: Sit in the Pose of a Child: Inhale – exhale, come off the heels rolling from the forehead onto the crown of the head, tucking the chin tightly into the notch of the throat, stretching the back to the neck – be aware of massaging the thyroid and para thyroid glands; inhale – return to Pose of a Child; keep the chest in touch with the thighs, raise the head – be aware of squeezing the back of the neck and stretching the throat. Repeat as often as you wish. Take care not to place too much pressure on the head – monitor this carefully.

Lie down – relax – take slow, deep breaths – sending Life Force to the head, neck and shoulders.

SPINAL ROLL: Lie on the back – draw the knees to the chest – cross the ankles – arms around the knees. Visualise a large clock face at the lower part of the spine – the 12 is at the base of the spine – the 6 is at the waist. Rotate the knees circling the perimeter of the clock face.

Inhale at the 12 – begin the exhalation going past the 3 till, arriving at the 6, the exhalation is completed. Inhale at the 6 – passing through the 9 till, arriving at the 12, the inhalation is completed.

Continue this with the eyes closed – face relaxed – visualising Life Force to flood the lumbar region of the spine.

SALUTE TO THE SUN

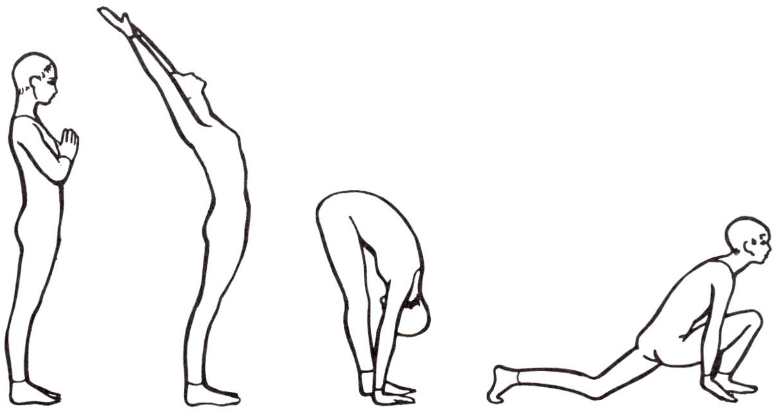

1.– Stand with feet slightly apart and parallel – hands in prayer position on the chest – elbows outward – spine erect – head slightly inclined forward.

2.– Exhale – inhale – raise both arms overhead and outward – bending slightly back.

3.– Exhale – bend down while stretching forward, leading with the chin – keep the knees straight – place the hands on either side of the feet – bring the head toward the legs.

If there are difficulties in placing the hands next to the feet while keeping the knees straight – just go as far as is possible and just before going on to 4 – bend the knees and place the hands on either side of the feet.

4.– Inhale – step back with the left foot – kneel on the left knee – look up while sinking the hips toward the floor.

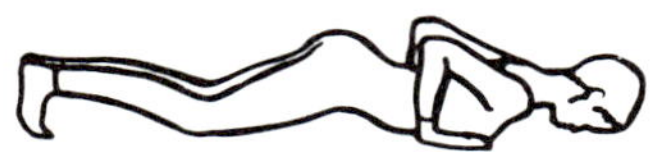

5.– Exhale – place the right foot next to the left foot – stretch back, pushing head and heels toward the floor. (Dog Stretch)

6.– Inhale – do not move the feet – place the knees to the floor – the chest between the hands – the chin to the floor.

7.– Exhale – do not move the knees – flatten the toes – flatten the body forward.

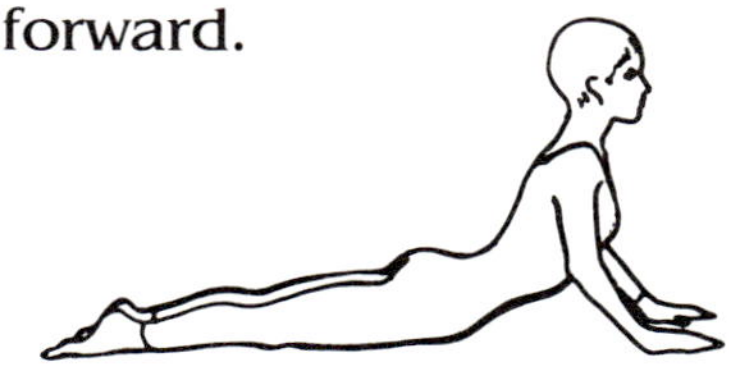

8.– Inhale – raise head and shoulders off the floor, coming up into Cobra – keeping the shoulders low.

9.– Exhale – tuck the toes under – back into Dog Stretch (see 5).

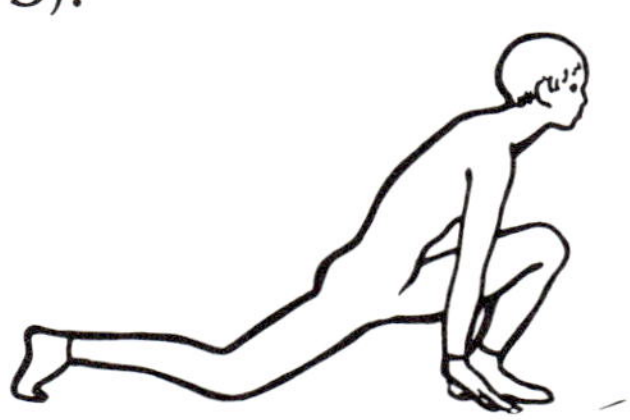

10.– Inhale – step forward with the left foot, placing it between the hands – kneel on the right knee – look up while sinking the hips to the floor (see 4).

11.– Exhale – place the right foot next to the left foot between the hands – straighten the knees – bring the head toward the legs (see 3).

12.– Inhale – raise both arms overhead – stretch back as in 2.

13.– Exhale – return to starting position (see 1).

Stand with the feet together and parallel – arms around the chest (left hand under right arm pit, right hand under left arm pit). Bend the head slightly forward – eyes are closed. Take a few slow deep breaths, calming the heart beat and the breathing before starting on the next round.

For the second round use the opposite side of the body – i.e. left foot instead of right foot, left knee instead of right knee.

SHOULDER STAND

This is sometimes called the Candle Pose. The movement is the same throughout as for the Half Shoulder Stand, except instead of holding the hips in the hands, the hands are placed high on the back, tucking the chin tightly into the notch in the throat. Bring the legs up so that the body is a straight line from the shoulders to the toes.

While holding the posture, the awareness is in the thyroid and para thyroid glands – see Life Force streaming into that area.

Coming down is the same as for the Half Shoulder Stand.

Not suitable for people with high blood pressure.

STOMACH CONTRACTIONS – (UDDIYANA AND NAULI)

While it is most unorthodox to practise Uddiyana and Nauli lying down, I have found it extremely effective, both personally and while working with people with disabilities.

In my opinion Uddiyana and Nauli should be taught by a teacher. However the lying-down version is quite easy to understand.

I feel that there are several advantages in the lying-down version as compared to the classic standing or cross-legged position. First of all, there is no strain on the spine and with so many people suffering from spinal discomfort, this certainly should be worth considering. Secondly, the hands are free for checking purposes which is very important in the initial stages. One can feel with the hands whether the hollow in the abdomen is formed in the Uddiyana pose and whether there is any movement in the abdomen while practising Nauli.

We will only concern ourselves here with Uddiyana.

Lie flat on the floor (a bed is really too soft). Knees bent – feet apart and drawn up toward the body – knees apart. Inhale – raise the buttocks off the floor, pushing the abdomen up. Exhale – slowly lower the body to the floor. Make sure that the exhalation is complete. HOLD THE BREATH OUT while pulling the small of the back into the floor – pulling the tail under – tightening the sphincter muscles in the pelvic floor – pulling the chin into the notch in the throat and finally pulling the abdomen upward and inward.

Hold this posture as long as possible. Feel with the hands that there is a pear-shaped hollow – the biggest part of the pear in the abdomen and the top part of the pear in the area of the stomach between the floating ribs.

When there is need for air – take several deep breaths in and out through the nose while resting comfortably on the floor. Do NOT begin another contraction till the breath is back to its normal rhythm.

At first repeat the above two times – slowly building up to six contractions.

It is essential that the breath is held OUT during the contraction as any air held in may cause pressure in the head.

Caution: People with heart trouble, lung disease or hyper tension (high blood pressure) should not practise the contractions without the consent of their medical adviser.

STRETCHES ON THE FLOOR

1.– Lie flat on the back, arms by the sides, feet together. Inhale – take the arms overhead to the floor, point the toes away from the head and stretch for as long as possible on the held breath; exhale, relax the arms by the sides. Take a deep breath in and out sending Life Force to the spine. Repeat three times.

2.– Same position, same stretch, except the feet are pointing toward the head, the feet flexed. Stretch into the heels. Repeat three times.

3.– Same position, feet flexed. Inhale – stretch the arms overhead, arms close to the floor; exhale, **hold the arms there** and raise the head just a little way off the floor; inhale – return the head to the floor; exhale, relax the arms by the sides. Take deep breaths till the breath has settled back to normal, sending Life Force to spine and shoulders. Repeat two times.

4.– Same position, feet pointing away from the head. Inhale – bring the arms overhead close to the floor; exhale, **hold the stretch, do not go limp;** inhale – stretch a little further; exhale, hold the stretch. Repeat this several times using your own judgement as to how far you want to stretch. When you feel the need to do so, lower the arms on an exhalation; shrug the shoulders; take them off the floor a few times and relax, take slow breaths, sending Life Force to the part of the body where you feel most affected by the stretch.

5.– Lie on the back – raise the right arm overhead – roll onto the right side of the body – ear resting on the arm – bring the left arm overhead – left hand on the right hand – head between the arms – legs straight – feet together.

Inhale – stretch the whole left side of the body – sliding the left hand past the right hand and the left foot past the right foot. **Do not raise the hand or foot** – SLIDE. Repeat three times.

Gently roll onto the back – bring the arms down – shrug the shoulders – take a few slow deep breaths. Other side.

If it is difficult to maintain steadiness while lying on one side – bend the knee of the leg which is on the floor – keeping the leg of the side which is stretching, straight.

This stretch is excellent to rectify an imbalance in the posture where one side of the body is identifyably shorter than the other.

Deep breathing – sending Life Force to the most affected area of the body.

SQUAT

Squat on your heels – feet as wide apart as possible – toes pointing outward – heels on the floor – hands in prayer position on the chest with the elbows touching the insides of the knees.

Inhale – exhale – press the palms of the hands firmly together – bring the hands down thereby separating the knees; inhale – return the hands to starting position. Repeat several times.

If keeping the heels on the floor presents difficulties, stand with your back against a wall – feet well apart – toes pointing outward – heels sixteen to twenty centimetres away from the wall – using the wall for support – slowly sink into the posture.

Deep breathing while in the posture – directing Life Force to the place in the body where you feel most affected.

TWISTS LYING ON THE FLOOR

1.– Lie flat on the back, arms out sideways at shoulder level, palms to the floor. Make sure to keep the knees together and the arms and shoulders to the floor throughout.

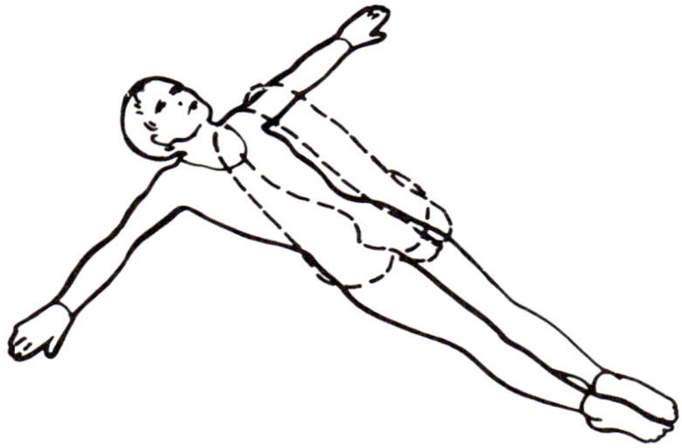

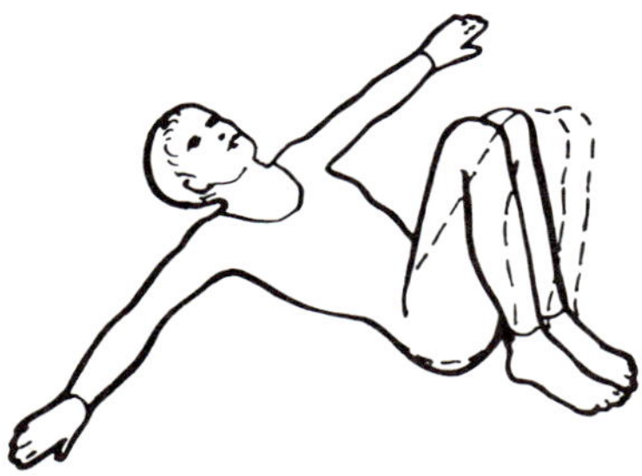

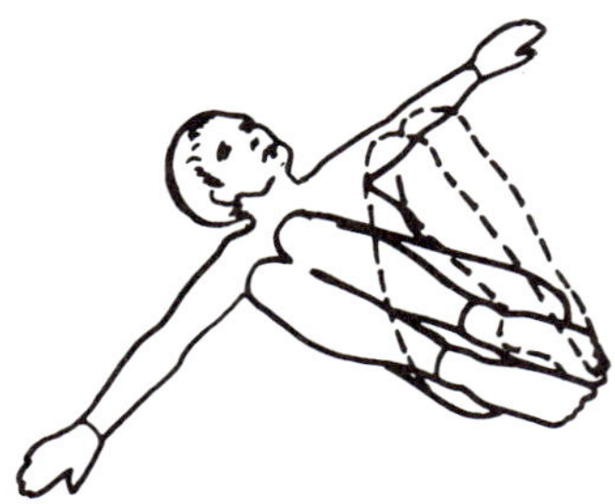

Inhale – exhale, bend the knees and draw them to the chest; inhale – exhale, take both knees toward the right upper arm; inhale, both knees back to the centre; exhale, both knees toward the left upper arm; inhale, centre. Repeat three times.

Return the legs to the floor; take slow deep breaths, sending Life Force to the spine.

2.– Lie flat on the back, arms out sideways at shoulder level, palms to the floor. Make sure to keep arms and shoulders to the floor throughout. Bend the knees and place the feet to the floor, heels close to the body – then separate the feet about 30 centimetres. Inhale – exhale, take both knees to the right; stay there for an in – and exhalation feeling the stretch; inhale – knees back to the centre; exhale, take both knees to the left; stay there for an in – and exhalation; inhale – centre. Repeat this three times.
Return the legs to starting position; take slow deep breaths, sending Life Force to the spine.

TRIANGULAR REST POSE

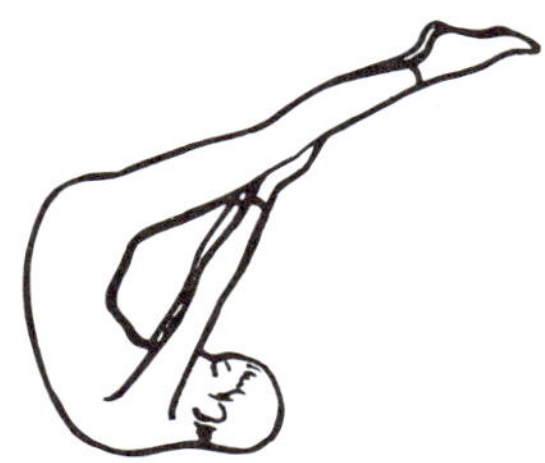

Same beginning as Half Shoulder Stand. In this posture we support the knees with the hands – elbows straight – balancing on the shoulders. Keep the breath flowing rhythmically – feeling the calm take a hold with each breath. Beneficial for people troubled by insomnia.

Coming down is the same as for the Half Shoulder Stand. Take slow deep breaths, sending Life Force to the spine.

Not suitable for people with high blood pressure.

INDEX

PART 1

Preface by Michael Volin
Foreword by Howard Kent
Introduction 1
Chapter 1 – How I became involved 4
Chapter 2 – Yoga as a Life Style 9
Chapter 3 – I could never do that 15
Chapter 4 – Breath, the Source of Life 19
Chapter 5 – Not too much Distress about Stress 29
Chapter 6 – Man's easiest Road to Suicide 45
Chapter 7 – Me meditating? You must be kidding! 64
Chapter 8 – The laughing Yogi 78
Chapter 9 – It is never too late 85

PART 2

Introduction to Part 2 88
Some consideration before starting your Yoga practice 90
Early Morning Practice 92
Other opportunities to practise Yoga 94
Simple Healing Meditation 95
Longer Meditation 97
Air 99
Arthritis 100
Asthma 104
Bad Posture 111
Bad Skin 112
Bowel Upset – Diarrhoea – Vomiting 113
Chest Colds and Coughs 114
Constipation 114
Cramps – Tingling in Legs and Feet 116
Cystitis – Incontinence – Kidney Problems – Swollen Ankles 117
Diabetes 120
Diet 121
Drowsiness 123
Eyes 124
Feet 124

Haemorrhoids – Prolapse of Abdominal Organs –
Varicose Veins 125
Heart Complaints 127
Hypertension 128
Insomnia 129
Knees 130
Menopause 131
Migraine – Head ache – Distorted Vision 132
Multiple Sclerosis 134
Osteoperosis 136
Parkinson's Disease 138
Pregnancy 142
Shrinking as we grow older 146
Sinusitis 146
Sore Throat 147
Spinal Problems 147
Stiffness in Neck and Shoulders 149
Stomach Muscles (strengthening of) 150
Stroke 154
Vitamins 154
Water 156
Weight Reduction 156

PART 3
Alternate Nostril Breathing 158
Balancing Postures 159
Breathing Practice to discourage Chest Colds and Coughs 160
Breathing Technique to discourage Head Colds and Sinusitis 162
Camel and Simple Camel 164
Cat and Cat Stretch 165-166
Pose of a Child 166
Cleansing Breath 167
Cobra 169
Diamond Posture 169
Exercises to be done while lying in Bed 170
Fish and Simple Fish 176-177
Half Locust 178
Half Shoulder Stand 178
Pose of a Hare 179
Head to Knee Pose lying down 180
Lion and Rolling up of the Tongue 181
Lunge 182

Plough 182
Relaxation Pose 183
Rolls 183
Salute to the Sun 185
Shoulder Stand 187
Stomach Contractions 188
Stretches on the Floor 189
Squat 191
Twists lying on the Floor 191
Triangular Rest Pose 193

NOTES

NOTES